How To Get Rich...
By The Book

*The 14 Eternal Truths, as Old as Creation,
That Still Work in Business and Life Today*

John F. Beehner

By The Book Publishers
Jacksonville, Florida

©Copyright 1996 by John F. Beehner
By the Book Publishing
7785 Baymeadows Way, Suite 304
Jacksonville, Florida 32256

All rights reserved. Written permission must be secured from the publisher to use or reproduce any part of this book except for brief quotations in critical review or articles.
ISBN:
0-9655745-0-4
Library of Congress Catalog Number
96-095208
Printed in The United States of America

For additional copies phone toll free
888–847–3861

TABLE OF CONTENTS

Introduction: Truth and Consequences viii

CREATION TRUTHS

The Business of Building Character 3
A World of Change 17
A Higher Standard 27
One Nation Under God 39

SPIRITUAL TRUTHS

The Meek Shall Inherit 51
Failure Leads to Success 65
Words are the Seeds of Life 79
The Problem with Religion 91

MORAL TRUTHS

We are Family by Design 107
Life is a Gift to Cherish 117
Well Done Faithful Servant 131
Giving Touches Both Hearts 143
Better to be a Poor Man, Than a Liar 153
Diversity is a Strength 165

The Bottom Line 181

Bibliography 189

Appendix 195

How to get Rich... By the Book

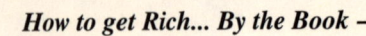

Acknowledgments

Many people have given me encouragement and support in making this book possible. I am sincerely thankful for their help. It would have been impossible without them. I want to recognize as many of them below as possible.

I especially want to thank God for leading me to and through every inch. My prayer is that this book will accomplish His purposes. I also want to say a special thanks to my wife Judy who has supported me and who has been very understanding. I will love her all the days of my life. In addition to the many who contributed personal stories and who are mentioned in the contents, I want to salute the following people as **"Encouragers"**.

Al Bertani, Jim Bleech, Jim Brewer, Bennett Brown, Nita Carr, John Cavanagh, Mark Charboneau, Sandy Fisher, Bill Hopf, Gary Howe, Pat Kelly, Chip MacGregor, Bill McCombes, David Miller, Dan Murphy, Larry Nichols, Tom Noton, Norb Novocin, Dr. Victor Oliver, Frank Orlando, John Rumbach, Charles "Red" Scott, Jay Strack, Steve Strang, Jeanie Tebeau, Billie Tucker, Jarda & Sara Tusek, Frost Weaver, and my mom and dad.

The following people have been **supporters** and deserve recognition as well:

Kelli Bass, Deanna Berg, Denny Brown, Susan Carlson, Arthur Carnes, Bud Carter, Larry Cassidy, Peter Chamberlain, Tom Crimm, Joe Day, Howard Dayton, Jerry Deley, Jim Dodd, Steve Douglass, Bob Downing, Larry Elliott, Christi Foster, Teresa Foster, Gary Gibbs, Bob Grano, Ben Goldsmith, Steve Gyland, Bill Hall, Steve Hall, Dennis Hensley, Susan Hill, Rick Houcek, Bob Jackson, Ron Jenson, John Johnson, Kouri, Jon Krug, Pete Lackey, Paul Landry, Frank Maguire, Joe Marino, John McCollister, Col. Nimrod McNair, Jim Miller, Ray Miller, Bobby Mitchell, Jack Mitchell, David Moore, Cork Motsett, Randy Overfield, Ken Overman, Buddy Pilgrim, Loren Rozeboom, Mick St. Jean, Larry Schneider, David Smith, Ted Sprague, Dan Stanley, Gil Stricklin, Peter Sullivan, Jeanie Tebeau, Pete Tinesz, John Vandiest, Ken Vensel, Frank Voehl, Denis Waitley, Don Wass, Kell Williams, Kathy Yanni, Dennis Zink, City of Jacksonville Public Library, and First Baptist Church Library, Jacksonville, Florida.

PREFACE

"It was just before dinner at our annual International Conference of peers of a business that I had devoted my life to for 12 years. People from around the world had gathered and probably 25 of the nearly 150 Executives there would be recognized for different accomplishments. I had got to my knees to say a quick prayer before I left for dinner. I was a little tense thinking that I might get a special award and had prepared nothing to say should it be given to me. In the prayer I said, *'Lord, am I going to get this award?'* Then I heard a small still voice say, *'No.'*"

I spent the early part of my career chasing the American dream as I understood it, wanting to have the riches of money, power and recognition. I was what people called a "moral person" who was enthusiastic, hard working, and a visionary. I had moved my family five times in ten years, always looking for greener pastures, moving to bigger successes, not really recognizing that I was on a false quest for the "world's view" of success. I had a basic belief in God but could see no relevance of Him in my life. I felt if I was just a good person that one day we would meet in Heaven.

But in starting my second business I was struggling. I had an incredible experience or a "divine intervention" and I surrendered my life to His leading. He led me to a business that works with CEOs of companies with a give-and-take, round-table approach using outside speakers, combined with a one-on-one process. It was the most outstanding and practical business experience anyone could ask for. I learned more through that process than many people will learn in two lifetimes. At the same time, I was effective enough to create a licensed business with a staff of 20, over 250 clients and associates.

Through the journey I became personally involved with some of the most successful entrepreneurs and had an opportunity to learn from their experience. This gave me a very broad understanding of how businesses effectively work.. I learned to put my faith in Him. After years of success, I later came to realize that I was off course from His leading. I called it God's wake-up call. I had much more to learn about my faith in Him and how to probe the "deeper" things about success and life's purposes.

Preface

"After dinner that same night in my hotel room while removing my jacket, I can remember it as if it were right at this moment — I said, *'Lord, how come I didn't get that award?'* Then a small soft voice responded, *'Because you are too prideful to think you should receive it and they are too prideful to give it to you.'* That answer sunk deep into my heart and I understood. The voice continued, *"You need to write a book on this."* And I said, *"A book, no...a chapter, maybe."*

Here I am over a year later having sold the majority interest in my business and having prayed, labored and researched the book you are now reading. Let me make one thing very clear...I am a messenger and not an author. He is the author and I have just done my best to be humble and open enough to be led to share the contents of the foundational truths that not only affect business but dictate our personal lives. I'm not patient or detailed enough to do this without Him teaching and grinding me. It has been both a big "stretch" and honor to do this.

- John Beehner

INTRODUCTION

TRUTH AND CONSEQUENCES

Riches Are Deeper Than Money

This book is about "panning for gold"...how to obtain the riches that we all seek through our personal and business lives.

Rich has 12 different definitions in Webster's New World Dictionary. Yes...the first relates to possessions, money or property. However, the other 11 refer to resources, values, workmanship, flavor, voice, soil, and other properties, while the most often used word is **abundance**. The purpose of this book is **not** to focus on money or possessions, but highlight the foundational truths for success. This book is about obtaining the **riches** of life that our Creator has planned for each of us.

Our level of understanding and obedience to His truths will impact our ability to pursue and obtain all types of riches. Yet most of us seek something deeper, more meaningful, long term and the eternal for their lives. Real riches are dependent upon receiving an inner peace of mind, personal sense of joy, sense of fulfillment and real understanding of the purpose of our life.

> "Success in life is not about acquiring wealth,
> but becoming rich from the inside out."

The Book

The truths and principles of this book are drawn from the Bible. They were recorded by Moses nearly 4,000 years ago.

The Bible has proved to be entirely credible by archaeologists, historians, prophecy, and through the presence of Christ. The Old Testament has many prophecies of Jesus coming....from where He was

Introduction

to be born and how He would die. The Bible is the most respected and best read book in the world. Between 1930 and 1987, 2.5 billion Bibles were sold in 300 languages. That is an average of 26 million Bibles a year. In the United States, the American Bible Society estimates that in 1991 there were 44 million Bibles sold in Christian bookstores alone (their organization alone donated 2 million Bibles that same year). Estimates could be as high as 60 to 70 million Bibles sold or given away each year by countless organizations or ministries. It is also estimated that one in five Americans buys a Bible each year.

Yet, many of us see the Bible as historical with a number of positive phrases or statements but little relevance to us. Once an individual makes a commitment to the **author** and **himself** to use the Bible for learning and enrichment, they are changed from the inside out. Their spirit starts to come alive and seeks a deeper relationship with our Creator.

The Bible is God's *"owner's manual"* to be used by each of us. The closer we come to understanding His word, the more we recognize the riches and abundance derived from His truths.

"Truth is truth, whether we believe it or not."

What is Truth?

God is a spirit of love, truth and light.
Truths are the highest form of law, principles, or foundations.
Jesus brought the spirit of the truth
(a deeper insight into the purpose of each law).
Note appendix on 14 Truths.

His Design

The reason our Creator gave us these truths was to give us a clearer path to maximize our experience here on earth and beyond. With the world filled with both good and evil, He knew our capabilities, body strength, resolve, mental capacity, spiritual depth and tolerance. By His design of us He knew what would make us happy and motivated to achieve His purposes. He is a loving father wanting the best for each of His children.

Yet, he loved us so much that He sent His only son to die for our mistakes, misunderstandings, lack of listening, ignorance and disobedience. Accepting Him as our Savior brings spiritual depth to our lives. We are first spirit, then body and soul. We can all live and work using only two out of our three cylinders in life. Too many of us miss the spiritual cylinder which is the most important part of our lives. The Bible says, *"God is spirit and the man without the spiritual relationship does not accept things that come from the spirit of God, for they are foolishness to him and he cannot understand them, because they are spiritually discerned."*

His truths work for all who obey them whether they are good or evil people. So may are confused because they believe they are operating on all cylinders as moral and good people.

This book is about understanding His design, His guideposts and warranties for a fulfilling life.

"You can't change the wind's direction, but you can change the sail."

Two Tracks...Which Do We Choose?

Our **first** choice is to continue on our own "self-created" track...playing the game of life on our terms, by our own **will**. At first examination this is the more appealing, enticing or attractive. It is the broader track with more "bells and whistles." It is a path reliant on the teaching of parents, friends, business and our society. If we have chosen the right truths from all those who have shared with us, we will have achieved specific successes and accomplishments by outward appearances. Yet, our hardest lessons are learned through circumstances or painful experiences spelled STRESS. Our ultimate goal is our own personal pleasure. Unfortunately this track is wide, unstable and filled with places to derail in darkness. Many of us who have been on this

Introduction

"rocky" track finally realize that we spend as much time avoiding pain as seeking pleasure. This deceiving track always leads us back to square one, where God always seems to be offering us a new start to get on His track for our lives.

Our **second** choice is to pursue His "God-created" track customized for us. This track has some of the world's enticements and opportunities the same as the first self-created track. What is different is that the ride is much more peaceful, fulfilling and focused by His direction for our lives. For those of us who have sincerely committed and stayed on His track, there is a light on their path and covering which draws us closer to Him with a more meaningful purpose. Things become clearer, and life and business is more enjoyable with spiritual riches.

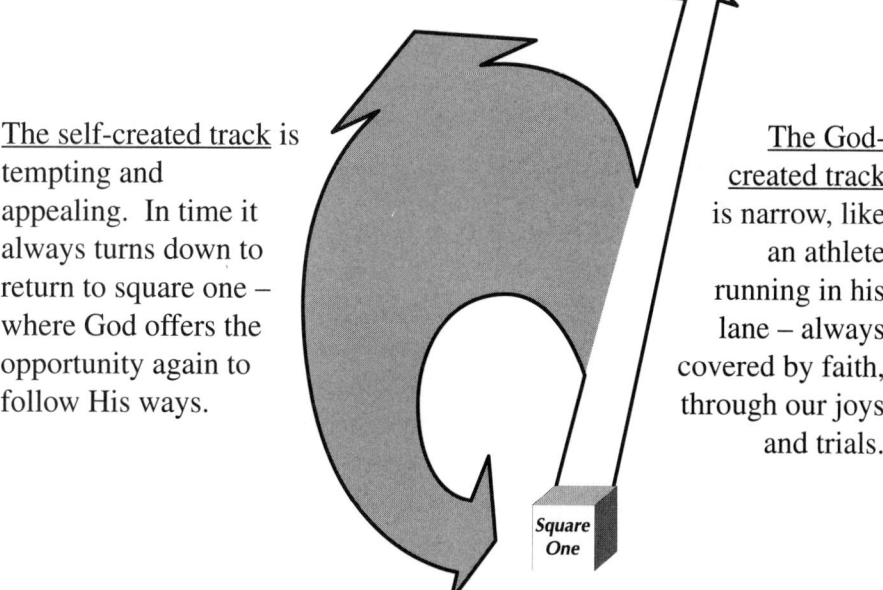

The self-created track is tempting and appealing. In time it always turns down to return to square one – where God offers the opportunity again to follow His ways.

The God-created track is narrow, like an athlete running in his lane – always covered by faith, through our joys and trials.

"Knowledge of truth is a more important form of currency than money."
Michael Kami

Pain and Healing

People with leprosy lose their nerve endings in their face, arms and legs and can easily break a finger or get burned without even knowing it. This is why lepers often have disfigured faces or only parts of fingers. Those who encounter the disease are often in prayer saying, *"Lord, please let me feel pain."* To them, pain is a gift from God. Most of us take it for granted and seek its avoidance.

Our Creator has a real purpose for pain, problems, frustrations and sacrifices as lessons in our life. Jesus died on the cross in pain for our pain as the ultimate sacrifice that God or any person could make. Pain can lead to humbleness, openness and convictions.

Our society has been leading us down a path that says the solution to pain, emptiness or stress is found in the "best" aspirin, beverage, entertainment, or even working harder. The same attitude is selling us on pain avoidance for the "wake-up calls" and trials of our lives. We have been deceived into dealing with symptoms rather than root causes. We may be trapped in a society that has lost its nerve endings and can't differentiate between **joy** and **pain** or **rich** and **poor** or **good** and **bad** because they have missed the difference between **truth** and **deceit**.

Generations before us never had the opportunity to pursue so many false idols or fixes. The founding fathers of America are an excellent example of a generation that sought spiritual and moral truths to solve their problems and guide their way. God wants to lead us and answer our prayers. Spiritual and moral solutions are the foundational answers to all of our needs. Whether we believe in Him or not, God is interacting in all of our lives every day either through:

1. His truths (and our obedience or avoidance of them).
2. Spiritual direction
3. Individual or group blessings.

"You cannot break the laws of God, you can only break yourself against them."

Introduction

The Eternal Life

Life is a test, a challenge and a journey. It does not end with our physical death. The spirit and the soul live beyond this earthly life. Obeying His eternal truths transcends our physical presence on earth and determines where we spend our next life. This requires changing our perspective from short term to long term, from our small selfish picture to the big picture, and from our perspective to His perspective. Our real riches come in our next life, dependent on our score in this one.

CREATION TRUTHS

In the book of Genesis in the Bible, God revealed the creation of heaven and earth and His creation of man and woman in His own image. He gave us dominion over earth expecting us to be fruitful...to take the initiative of sowing, growing and reaping, using our God given talents by the sweat of our labor. Finally, He told us to rule over every living creature...leading by example over the physical and mental aspects of life.

Ultimately He still rules over the spiritual world which we must learn to interact with to achieve His purposes and receive a peaceful and fulfilling life.

These Creation Truths coupled with the proper application of the Moral Truths are the foundational keys to the ongoing success of business.

How to get Rich... By the Book

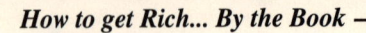

THE BUSINESS OF BUILDING CHARACTER

Creation Truth: *God Created Man In His Image*

Character Quality: *Take on My Character of Love*

Could Cancer Be A Blessing?

Few sports fans will ever forget the performance of Dave Dravecky of the San Francisco Giants baseball team a few years ago. Because of cancer, part of his left pitching arm had to be removed. He made a well-publicized comeback only to break his arm in the second game. The cancer had returned and the family agreed with the doctor that the best decision was to amputate his arm.

Today Dave says, *"Cancer has been a blessing. God has given me an opportunity to share His love with so many different people because of my circumstances. You know a valley for a farmer is a very rich place to plant a crop. When we go through the valleys of life, it is very rich for each of us. Unfortunately, my pride got in my way. I just wanted to be in control. But through my suffering I have become more like Him. He shapes us and molds us in the way he wants us to be. Suffering produces perseverance... perseverance produces character... and character produces hope. Hope will not disappoint us through and with Him. We are all in-process. He is the healer. Through this experience I have learned to look at life from an eternal perspective."*

"I thank God for my handicaps, for through them, I have found myself, my work and my God."

Helen Keller

CHARACTER QUALITY

- Take on My Character of Love-

The word character originates from a Greek word that means to "chisel." You mold your character by how you respond to circumstances and people. Take on my character of love.

In 1728, Benjamin Franklin was on a personal quest. With all his study and research, he concluded that happiness should be our ultimate goal in life and that it could only be attained through correct actions. He picked 13 virtues that he would do his best to live by each day. He developed a score card he used each day. He exemplified the men of character that shaped our national future who believed in honesty, humility, justice and the Golden Rule. Today, many live by the philosophy of "me-ism," my rights, self interest, quick fixes, and the short-cut to personal success, without sincere regard for others.

Our creator is calling us to take on His image, nature and character of **Love** (toward Him and one another), **Truth** (His principles), and **Light** (His path for our lives). As we do these things, we honor Him.

The number one purpose of a business is not to make a profit, but to take on and exemplify His character to others. Unless we know Him intimately and follow His ways, we are destined to learn through circumstances and trials. If we heed these experiences, we will eventually learn His ways and our character will come closer to His image.

Working the Principle

J. C. Penney's father was a farmer and a pastor, while his mother was a devoted homemaker in a small town in Missouri. During his early retail experience he was offered a partnership in a new store in Kemmerer, Wyoming, known as The Golden Rule Store. Little did he know that the principle *"Do unto others as you would have them to do unto you,"* he learned from his father and early partners would set the tone for a retail business still flourishing today.

He would later say it was the teaching of his parents that said, *"When a man works with a principle, that principle makes him representative of a great working force. He need never be anxious. The creative power of the universe is behind him. He is working not for anyone, but a principle is working for him, his success is assured."*

As he began to employ people and lay down his principles, he came to the conclusion that *"Making money must always be a by-product of building the character of men and women and the rendering of essential service to mankind."*

Changing Lives

Truett Cathy is considered a "non-conformist" in business circles because of his convictions and character. In 1946, he founded Chick-Fil-A, a $400 million company that does its very best to live by its principles and beliefs. Truett openly shares what he thinks are the three key ways we can "change lives" of those we lead, manage or just interact with:

1. By our instruction: what we say.
2. By our influence: what we do.
3. By our image: what we are and what we stand for.

In other words, changing lives takes precedence over making money. Profit is merely a by-product of producing good people.

Chick-Fil-A is one of the few retail businesses located in malls throughout the country that is closed on Sundays because he still believes in observing the Sabbath and encouraging employees to grow spiritually. Truett has been teaching Sunday School to 13-year-olds for 40 years. Not long ago an attorney from Atlanta, who was in his class as a teen told him, *"I remember very little about what you said in Sunday School but I do remember that you brought me some chocolate pudding to my house when I was sick."* Truett continued, *"He remembered what I did. Kids, like adults, will copy us. We all teach character and values at work as well as at home."*

He reminded his listeners, *"We are created in the image of God and it is up to us to do our very best in all our circumstances. I tell young people, it is a do-it-yourself world. You can't blame your parents for your circumstances."* We all start from an uneven playing field/life doesn't always seem fair.

The Real Dream

History will never forget the passionate speech of Martin Luther King when he said, *"I have a dream that my four little children will one day live in a nation where they will not be judged by the color of their skin but by the content of their character."* For each of us it becomes a question of finding our higher purpose, then we must allow God to build our character, strengthen our spirit and inspire our love to pursue it.

Martin Luther King learned his character from his father and mother, their spiritual convictions and seminary. As we study his traits, we see that he exemplified the character and image of Christ. Jesus took the approach of loving, teaching and modeling truth, willing to sacrifice himself for the greater calling of God.

Had Martin not taken the Christian, non-violent approach, he would have never found his place in history and made great progress for his people. His approach serves as another example for all of mankind that love will always win over hate.

"Ability will help a man to go to the top, but it takes character to keep him there."

Role Models

Charles Barkley, the great NBA star, said by TV commercials, "I am not your kid's role model." Like it or not kids with or without a father have for years idolized athletes. It used to be that media did not hunger to report the negative or criminal activities of heroes. Today it is front page news as a result of the erosion of values, character traits and the pursuit of negative news.

Reggie White, the outstanding NFL football player and ordained preacher is a man who has used both his influence and money to "walk his talk." He has been an inspiration to thousands, an individual we can all look up to. Reggie said, *"Playing football is helping me in my spiritual life. It is helping me build character. People cry out for role models. The problem is that in our society a lot of our kids are choosing the wrong heroes. We should be looking for the ones who have character, the ones who seek Him and humble themselves to a higher calling and a superior being. They are the ones who are going to have a stronger character than probably anybody you will meet."*

The Corporate Coach

Jim Miller is CEO of a $100 million office supply firm that has 57% market share in the Dallas/Fort Worth area. He authored a highly respected and practical book called <u>The Corporate Coach</u>. When you get face-to-face with Jim and ask him what motivates him to still be in his business he says, *"It is the fact that I just love to see people grow and develop their character and aptitudes. That's what thrills me. I have seen hourly people grow from young and inexperienced to vice-presidents and partners in the company. I refuse to be called CEO*

If You Knew The Future

If God gave you His plan for your future, how would you react? Jim Brewer, business counselor, says, "Most of us would say, but God, I can't do that. I'm not qualified."

So He leads us one step at a time until our character and confidence develops... until we finally discover and realize this is what I'm supposed to do."

The wise person then stops to reflect and thank God for the journey... and for not telling them what they would not believe.

because my real job is being the **coach**. *If you love, care, grow and counsel people, help them stretch themselves and develop their character, the sales and profits will follow."*

Character:
*"Our strength is shown in the things we stand for;
Our weakness is shown in the things we fall for."*

Hiring Smart

Red Scott is an icon in business, one of those unique individuals and personalities who took a $30 million business to $2 billion in 15 years, yet he took time to humbly share his cardinal principles with thousands of business executives throughout the country.

His expertise was in mergers and acquisitions — growing companies for future sale, so hiring Presidents of companies became critical as they bought businesses. He said, *"We were looking for superstars in 'game-breaker' positions (just like a key position on an athletic team, such as a great quarterback or linebacker, that could make or break the ability of a team to win). At that level we were doing our best to* **hire smart** *by putting candidates through intensive interviewing and screening processes. One of the most over-riding qualities we looked for in individuals was the level and maturity of their character. I am gun-shy to hire people who have not been through significant learning experiences in their life and bounced back–what some people would call 'the school of hard knocks.' Candidates without the right character qualities were the first to be screened out."*

Red Scott and Sam Walton were among the few high profile CEOs who have openly acknowledged their belief in God and that they believe that a faith in God and regular worship is critical to an executive's character.

*"Who you are is more important
than what you know."*

Ed Ryan

The Risk Takers

In 1959, Ada, Michigan became the birthplace of a company that does over $5 billion, offering over 10,000 quality products and services through nearly a million worldwide distributors. Rich DeVos and Jay Van Andel pioneered a multi-level industry and are estimated to have helped more people start their own small businesses than anyone else in the world.

Amway's first credo states that: *"We believe that every man, woman and child is created in God's image and because of that each has a worth, dignity and unique potential. Therefore, we can dream great dreams for ourselves and others!"*

While 80% of American small businesses fail in 5 years, these risk takers create the majority of jobs every year. Nothing builds character faster in an individual than starting his own business. We all have talents, but not all the talents we need to be successful alone. Small business offers the opportunity for individual initiative and fuels risk-taking, innovation, competition, pricing and niche marketing. It stretches people to come to grips with their desires, will and determination...all spiritual traits which God uses to further our character growth for a higher purpose.

The Winningest Coach

Only one man has been inducted in the Basketball Hall of Fame as both player and coach. After coaching for 40 years and winning 82% of his games, he said that winning isn't everything. He used all of his abilities and resources to help mold young men into individuals of character. He taught the principles of fair play, integrity, respect, discipline (teaching his players to leave basketball on the court) and living a balanced life.

John Wooden shared this creed with his players and fellow coaches:

1. *Be true to yourself / your talents and convictions.*
2. *Make each day your masterpiece / doing your best.*
3. *Help others because it is better to give.*
4. *Make friendship a fine art.*

5. Build a shelter for a rainy day trusting Him and others.
6. Drink deeply from The Good Book and others each day.
7. Every day pray for guidance and give thanks.

How could one coach from UCLA be so consistent and win more championships than anyone else in history? Because his simple values came from the right source of knowledge and truth. Was he wise or blessed, or both?

> *"He is more interested in making us what we ought to be than in giving us what we think we ought to have."*

Hard Lessons

Joe Gibbs, the Hall of Fame and former football coach of the Washington Redskins, shares publicly how God has worked through his life. During the earlier tenure of his time in Washington he decided that he needed to be an "aggressive businessman" during the off season to be able to make money for his future security and personal wealth. He said, *"I got into an Oklahoma land deal. It personally 'wiped me out.' It was against my wife's better judgment and without prayer that I made the decision. Unfortunately it was my pride and ego. I learned more about myself during that time. God built my character and He loved me through it all and miraculously I avoided bankruptcy and publicity."* The lesson Joe learned was that he had not known or focused on God's plan for his life. Sometimes these lessons are expensive and take us to the brink.

A New Start

Shortly after the fall of the Iron Curtain, the Russian Ministry of Education asked Campus Crusade For Christ and a number of other American ministries to help their teachers and students acquire the principles that seem to make America great. Ironically they told the Russians that they would have to allow the Bible in the classroom. Without much hesitation, the Russians complied and a new ministry called "Co-

Mission" was created. Over three thousand Russian teachers have been trained by 350 American volunteers who spend anywhere from three weeks to a year training teachers and assisting in the classrooms. Their mission is called "Character Training," taking the principles from the Bible to teach and share about honesty, integrity, commitment, initiative, and self-discipline. The program has received so much notoriety and success that many Americans are asking their public school districts to do the same.

> *"Adversity helps us grow."*
> **Tom Osborne**

Turnaround

In the 70's, Bob Rosof, a successful contractor, had retired to his boat in Tampa Bay, Florida. He was asked by a judge (and personal friend) to take a teenager on board to determine what he could do to help turn him around rather than send him to jail. Today, Bob is again retired from Associated Marine Institute, the organization he created, and which continues to work in 42 national locations to help turn around the lives of approximately 2500 young adults who have been sentenced by courts. The story of Associated Marine Institute is a well-documented one. It has been reported by national television, featured in <u>Parade</u> magazine and has received national media coverage when American presidents came to visit. Because of the efforts of AMI, 80% of the kids stay out of jail. The program builds the character they never received at home.

> *"A man wrapped up in himself makes a very small package."*

Character First

Over the last twenty years the oil industries have had a number of booms and busts which have made it very difficult for Tom Hill to keep his people motivated to the highest level of productivity and quality. Tom Hill runs Kimray, a $25 million, third generation manufacturing firm with 250 people in Oklahoma City. They manufacture regulators and control valves for the oil industry. More than the ups and downs of the business, Tom noticed the attitudes and work ethics of those he hired never seemed to be as good as years earlier.

He began to work with Bill Gothard of the Institute for Basic Life Principles in Oak Brook, Illinois, and they developed a program called Character First. They identified 49 Biblical character traits (some might call them attitudes) that apply to everyday life such as: wisdom, flexibility, punctuality, thoroughness, initiative, dependability, compassion and loyalty. Their belief is that people will repeat behavior that is praised, as taught in Ken Blanchard's "One Minute Manager" approach of "catching people doing things right." Over the last four years employees have been recognized in monthly company meetings, not for their individual performance, but for exhibiting special character contributions to the company's success. Supervisors present the awards and describe the character exhibited by the individual. As their concept developed they started using the same traits in their hiring practices.

The concept seems to be working because personnel problems are down 80%, margins are up, sales are up, profits are at record levels, while cost of raw materials and labor have increased significantly. They had an 80% reduction in worker's compensation costs and employee bonuses last year were 12.5% of their annual salaries. Kimray has dropped its quality control program and become a leader in its industry by having the highest warranties and fewest returns.

But even more satisfying to Tom Hill is the morale difference that he notices in his people.

He believes that **his purpose is to honor his creator and use his business to serve his employees and their families in building their character, strengthening them as individuals and nurturing their household**. No, he hasn't forgotten the customer or making a profit... they are just not #1 in his list of priorities (they are #1A).

He has also begun a movement to teach other companies how to adopt these principles in their own businesses. Tom says, *"Character and attitude start from within a person's heart, so they are more fundamental than attempting to manipulate behavior from the top down. Many people today are not taught the same character traits in the home as they were in the 1950's. It is part of our purpose and what God has laid on my heart to do. We've got to do our part to rebuild America's fiber."*

*"He is holy and does not conform to a standard,
He is the standard."*

Humbleness Leads To Character

Through the annals of history, God always seems to use the humble to accomplish eternal tasks. Why does He only use the humble (open, teachable, listeners) and obedient?

Because they are not saddled by material wealth, self-grandizing or the entrapments which block their spirit from hearing His voice.

Here are a few examples of the humble who have changed the world:

Noah	Joseph
12 Disciples	Abraham
Moses	Martin Luther King, Jr.
Billy Graham	Mother Teresa
Henry Ford	Joan of Arc
George Washington	Ben Franklin
Ronald Reagan	Abraham Lincoln
Knute Rockne	Alexander Graham Bell
Albert Einstein	Gandhi
Dag Hammarskjöld	Helen Keller
Pope John Paul	Norman Vincent Peale
James Madison	Albert Schweitzer
Winston Churchill	Bill Bright
James Dobson	Robert Schuller
Franklin Roosevelt	Dwight Eisenhower
Walt Disney	

Paradoxes of a Person of God

Strong enough to be weak;
Successful enough to fail;
Wise enough to say, "I don't know";
Right enough to say, "I'm wrong";
Compassionate enough to discipline;
Mature enough to be childlike;
Planned enough to be spontaneous;
Great enough to be anonymous;
Stable enough to cry;
Leading enough to serve.

Barry Morrow

"The Closer we come to Him, the more we become like Him."

THE MORAL OF THE STORIES

1. We are to learn from our circumstances, handicaps and adversity to take on His image, nature and character... in preparation for an eternal life.

2. We are not created to be alone. He loves us and wants to be loved in return through our journey. That is the simple purpose of life.

3. We all teach character, values and attitudes by what we say and do, at home and also in business, employment settings where the majority of adults spend the greatest share of their waking hours.

4. Character is defined in the Bible through Scripture, stories, examples and parables. His image is love, truth and light.

5. For many of us, we have a hard time breaking out of our

"comfortable lifestyle." He is asking each of us to depend on Him to take on the risk of His character traits each day. We are constantly in character development, all lifelong. If we listen, He speaks through these circumstances.

6. People with the right character are more teachable and reach toward the depths of life.

> ### *Answers To Prayer*
>
> *Per business counselor, Jim Brewer, prayer is answered by God in three ways:*
> - A. "Yes, I've been waiting for you to ask. This will be a good experience for you in preparation for My greater plan in your life.
> - B. No, this is not right for you.
> - C. Wait, your character and heart need to grow and mature."
>
> God looks at the motives of our prayers and actions, whether they are right or wrong for us. All of these answers build character and our faith.

7. Most employers say that their greatest assets are their people, however, they focus on profits to reach their goals and impress themselves and their stockholders. Profits come and go, but the character of people is eternal. Without the good character in our employees there is no customer. At the same time the customer is critical and profitability is vital to survive and grow a company. When the focus or priorities are askew, achieving eternal results are not in His image. We honor God when we honor His purposes and His people.

8. His image is long term. He is calling us to set aside the "quick fixes" and instant success shortcuts and desires of "the world" and look to His ways which may take longer because

we grow in character from the experience.

9. In my twenty years of owning, counseling and learning from successful CEOs, consultants and their experiences, I've concluded that culture and "walking the talk" are the most important internal factors in business productivity and the character of a company.

Character Defined

Leaders of companies teach character values by "walking their talk." Below are the 49 character traits "biblically based" that the Character Training Institute recommends for recognizing employees for demonstrating and contributing to a company's success:

Alertness	Faith	Patience
Attentiveness	Flexibility	Persuasiveness
Availability	Forgiveness	Punctuality
Boldness	Generosity	Resourcefulness
Cautiousness	Gentleness	Responsibility
Compassion	Gratefulness	Reverence
Contentment	Hospitality	Security
Creativity	Humility	Self-Control
Decisiveness	Initiative	Sensitivity
Deference	Joyfulness	Sincerity
Dependability	Justice	Thoroughness
Determination	Love	Thriftiness
Diligence	Loyalty	Tolerance
Discernment	Meekness	Truthfulness
Discretion	Obedience	Virtue
Endurance	Orderliness	Wisdom
Enthusiasm		

A WORLD OF CHANGE

Creation Truth: *Be fruitful and increase*

Character Quality: *By sowing, growing and reaping*

The Change in Communication

- In 1800 a letter sent coast-to-coast in America could easily take months by stagecoach to reach its destination.
- In 1860 it took several weeks by Pony Express.
- In 1869 it took a week or so by train.
- In 1920 that same letter took only a few days by plane.
- In 1960 it would overnight by jet.
- Since the mid 1980's, it took just a few seconds by FAX.
- Today we have instant communication through E-Mail plus same day delivery of hard copy information.

Technology is advancing so rapidly that information is globally accessible at lightning speed. The time required for one company to mirror or copy another company's products is exponentially faster than ever before. As a result, product life cycles are being shortened to radically brief periods of time. Changes are occurring at warp speed. Many predict that the FAX will be obsolete in the next 2 years because of the Internet.

"Plans are often worthless, yet the planning process is priceless."
Dwight Eisenhower

CHARACTER QUALITY

- Sow, grow and reap -

Life begins with a seed and passes through stages of personal or business growth with time tables for fruitfulness and harvest:

- to be prosperous for a year, grow wheat
- to be prosperous for ten years, grow trees
- to be prosperous for a lifetime, grow people
- to be prosperous for an eternity, grow close to God.

By His design, we are charged with taking the initiative, being self-starters and filling this earth with humankind. We are to use our creativity to make life better by ultimately bringing the world's brothers and sisters together as one with Him.

The cycles of change are unstoppable and time is irreplaceable. In the year, 1900, experts said knowledge would double every 100 years. Today world wide experts agree that knowledge is doubling every 2 years. Yet, our Creator gave us Truths so we may gain wisdom, knowledge and discernment..

We have natural, physical and spiritual laws. Sowing, growing and reaping is both natural and spiritual. Our abundance of fruitfulness in the world is by His design. Our world of rapid change is preparing us for something greater.

"Our Choices in Life are Between:
<u>No</u> where and <u>Now</u> here."

Frank Maguire

The Cycles of Change

In 1900, 95% of Americans lived off the land. By 1950, it was 15%. In the 1920's there were over 100 automobile manufacturers in the United States. By 1950, there were six. We've gone from Mom and Pop corner grocery stores to supermarkets to warehouse super stores.

In the mid 1970's, the leading manufacturer of portable calculators was Bowmar, and the average calculator sold for $125. By the mid 1980's, they were out of business and a calculator the size of a credit card sold for 80 cents. In the early 1980's, yogurt, computer and video stores were popping up in thousands of small strip retail centers around the country. Within 10-12 years, there were a handful of national companies controlling the market share.

Products and services are always moving in a cycle of innovation, start-up, rapid growth or failure, maturity, commodity and decline. These are the same cycles of life. All products eventually become commodities, so innovation is absolutely critical to stay even or get ahead.

"Without risk (faith), there is no growth."

The World Impact

What are the incredible events and circumstances

Resisting Change

The late Bill Oncken, great trainer on the principles of "Managing Management Time," says that "Most people go through life backing into the future, keeping their eyes on the past...the things they have been educated to do and done well. Rather than turn around and face the future and openly deal with the unknowns –accepting them as a challenge." There is a resistance in all of us to venture into some new territories. Yet, there is a spiritual guidance system that our creator put into each of us with the intent we would seek Him for confirmation – knowing our talents, capability and His purposes He placed within us.

that are causing changes to compound so rapidly? There are three driving forces:

1. One is technology derived from the reaping of the harvest from the American Space Program and other initiatives.
2. The second is driven by the changes in political events focusing around the fall of communism and impact on our defense spending.
3. The third is economics and increasing competition as the world is brought closer together.

As we observe these events and Biblical perspectives, a greater plan appears to be unfolding.

"Experience is always the hardest teacher, because you take the test before you learn your lesson."

Technology Explosion

By the year 2000 we will double the number of satellite transmitters to be able to instantaneously send pictures and data throughout the world. Cellular telephone communication will grow faster than any other medium as underdeveloped countries will use it rather than spending the time and money to establish underground or overhead wiring/cable replacing phone systems that are archaic and less reliable. Digital TV, digital sound and transmission will improve and increase communication dramatically.

More and more of us will run our own business from home and use our own satellite disk offering 500 channels from around the world!

Computer access is now world wide with data storage expanding because of increasingly smaller chips with greater capacity allowing PC computers to maintain entire libraries for internal and external use. Networking for inner office or inner company purposes will be maximized within the next few years tripling communication capacities. The Internet will not only provide communication for E-Mail, but home libraries and new areas to market and buy products world wide. We are just on the threshold of using these techniques.

"If you always do what you've always done, you will always get what you've always got."

Political Enlightenment

In 1988 Dr. Robert Thompson spoke to numerous CEO and entrepreneur groups while he served as a White House advisor. He boldly predicted that within a short time communism would fall. Why? Because of the technology revolution, through satellite and computer communication and that the "truth" would no longer be able to be withheld from the people in communist countries. He predicted an eventual overthrow of those governments. Few CEOs recognized the truth in his predictions, especially after almost 40 years of communist rule.

Today nearly 50% of the world's population has turned from communism or dictatorship toward "a free market economy." Only China maintains its communist government while moving rapidly toward free enterprise with the fastest economic growth of any nation in the world today. As the leaders of these economies continue to earn and understand free market concepts, they will copy American products and services at much lower costs, creating more competition world wide. By the year 2000, for Americans the idea of a smaller world and larger marketplace will be a reality.

Under communism the average individual in the Czech Republic earned under $1,000 per capita per year (communism was a form of welfare). Just six years since its new government, the average income is projected at $7,500.

Reduction of American armed forces has changed America's employment picture. The need has been to assimilate more returning servicemen, thus creating more jobs.

"When God measures a man, He puts the tape around the heart instead of his head."

Economic Consequences

Where will these new international businessmen go to learn about the free market economy? The United States is the most open society and the most prolific "giver" of information and knowledge. For years underdeveloped countries have sent their best and brightest to our prestigious schools. But this educational quest will be more of a grass roots business-to-business learning experience in the years to come.

- The information age produced a boom in business literature (books, magazines, tapes) for large businesses and small businesses over the last thirty years.
- Trade agreements such as NAFTA will grow as we protect our markets and start partnering more with foreign companies in strategic alliances, not only to share knowledge, but for economic growth opportunities.
- The American service sector took over from the manufacturing sector as the largest employer just a few years ago. We recognize that manufacturing jobs create more economic wealth and require more support employment. Just as the textile industry left Europe and England in the 1800's to move to the New England area of the United States, they also moved to the Carolinas in the 1900's. While many still maintain manufacturing in the United States, much of their production is done overseas in Southeast Asia or has been captured by foreign companies in those marketplaces importing into the USA The opportunity remains for small and mid size businesses in America to learn and expand their exporting efforts like big businesses have been doing for years. This is the great opportunity for us to be involved in a world marketplace. Yet many smaller entrepreneurs are too "spoiled" by many years of richness in an expanding American marketplace to take new risk in a world market.
- American business will continue to be caught up in the "margin games" to gain the edge and ability to compete worldwide when economics are so divergently different from our own. This puts economic pressures even on the

company that doesn't do business internationally. So downsizing and re-engineering will remain alternatives to American business leaders. Unfortunately some top executives are using downsizing and economic pressures as an excuse to "look good" to stockholders rather than doing what is right.

"The pilgrims gave us the legacy of faith to risk a better life. Today the faith to risk continues to lead people to start a business."

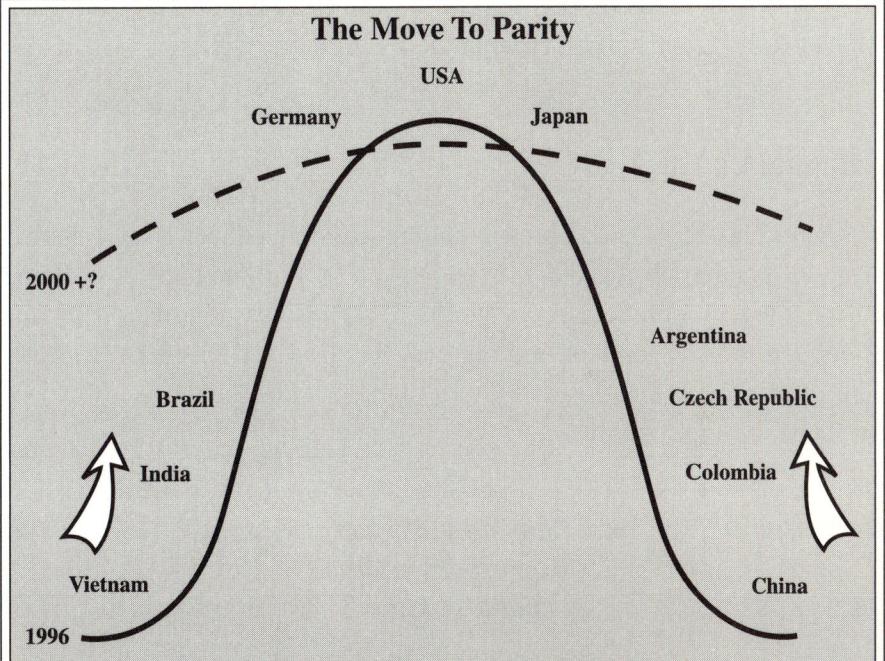

The Move To Parity

USA
Germany   Japan

2000 +?

Argentina
Brazil   Czech Republic
India   Colombia
Vietnam   China

1996

The world is moving toward parity. It is obvious that the United States, Japan and Germany rest near the top of the bell curve of economic prosperity and productivity. Many of the underdeveloped countries are moving up rapidly as they gain technology and have an understanding of how to do business in a free world marketplace. The value of the American dollar is going down while other currencies rise. Does that mean that by the year 2005 we will all be playing on a more even economic playing field? Yes, even though some countries may be left behind. The world's success depends upon adapting the moral truths of the Golden Rule in business and life. (This will be clear in Chapters 9-14.)

What is America's Role?

Interestingly enough America has been the greatest example of change and "being fruitful and increase" for the world. Much of this is exemplified through our innovations to market and sell products in an economical way. Most of the world uses the English word, "marketing," in their own language which was invented in the US Former communist countries are just learning what marketing really even means, since they formerly were part of "state planned economy." Our role will not only be to continue to teach the world the economic principles of a free market economy but to also teach the ethics from which its success is driven. Our ethics and character come from the Ten Commandments. So when we share ethics we will be sharing God's principles.

Bringing Us Together

As technology and its speed in communication, education and sharing bring us together as a world, the political and economic barriers of doing business together are reduced. In order to do business internationally, the American model based on morals must be used for long-term success. This moves the world closer to God's higher standard and opens the door for more spiritual growth.

"Sorrow looks back
Worry looks around.
Faith looks up."

THE MORAL OF THE STORIES

1. He did not say be dependent upon others or governments. He said take initiative and risks in order to be fruitful and fill the earth.
2. God is love, truth and light. With the fall of the Iron Curtain and as these countries work toward building their economic capacity to do business throughout the world, a major barrier

has fallen. A communist nation such as China who has been pirating, i.e., American videos and CDS will not continue to maintain these practices and have economic viability with the rest of the world. Those who lived under communism and a society of fear are now having to adjust their paradigms and mental thinking to understand the moral truths (i.e., faith is the opposite of fear, honesty is truth) that God set in motion to make the fair exchange of goods and services viable to everyone.

3. Businesses that continue to seek short term profitability may be sacrificing or gambling with God's eternal purpose for their business. The game of juggling the economics and accounting of a business often results in acquisitions to increase sales volume, cutting costs to translate that into profitability. Yet the long term future is most important. Tom Phillips, retired CEO of Raytheon, says that "The eternal view would help prevent fantasies of unlimited risk taking for corporations. The eternal view also keeps at bay personal feelings of total devastation when risks appear to be failing."

As we become a media driven society, the deceit we absorb hinders our convictions and God's desire to work through us. Our motives will catch up with us. God is looking at the long term and the truth of the heart...His goal is for us to be unselfish and not self-centered.

4. The myth that the "only constant is change" will divert our focus on reality. The truth is God is the only constant. He is the same yesterday, today and tomorrow. His truth is law. As we know Him, we change to become more like Him.

5. What really caused the dramatic fall of the Iron Curtain? There was barely a shot fired nor any significant loss of life. It was like a house of cards. It seemed to start with simple prayer in churches in Romania that had been closed for years. The pressures created by the Reagan administration certainly forced Russia to focus upon the economic realities. Did communism fall because of God's hand, the weight of its own sin, American pressure, or all of the above? In the end,

righteous will always win over evil.
6. Is the technology explosion because of man or God? God is facilitating this change to bring us closer together to prepare for His son's return. It is time for each of us to seek the owner's manual (Bible) and make our own determinations.
7. The Book of Revelation talks about a time similar to the one that we are experiencing. Those falling away from belief are being more critical and hypocritical while those coming closer are surrendering to Him. Our society is caught up in an interpretation of values and we are picking sides. Weekly church attendance in the U.S.A. is up to 45% vs. 39% in 1950.
8. A number of men study Bible prophecy. Grant Jefferies, a businessman from Toronto, Canada, says through his studies and research that there are 38 major Biblical prophecies which must be fulfilled before the return of Christ. As of 1996, all have been fulfilled or are in the process. Is He preparing a way for Jesus to return?

What Causes Our Frustration?

1. *Not enough of something? (money, status or love?)*
2. *Results from a bad decision we made?*
3. *No long term perspective for our future?*
4. *Or our violation of His Truths and their consequences?*

A HIGHER STANDARD

Creation Truth: *Fill and subdue the earth*

Character Quality: *By Putting Your Talents to Work*

Being the Best

Bill McCartney, as former head coach for the University of Colorado, won a national championship and has been credited for a new winning standard for their program. Now as Chairman of Promise Keepers, a national Christian men's movement, he often has an opportunity to address men in stadiums around the country and share some of his experiences as well as his walk with the Lord. He publicly shares how he used a method to "bring out the best" in his players once every few years. It was such an intense experience that it is not something that could be repeated often. But he says *"When we had to play a nationally ranked team where I just had to pull out all the stops, I would use this technique."*

He would tell all the players in a team meeting on Monday that he was going to be in his office on Wednesday and wanted to meet individually with each player for three minutes only. He said, *"Men, I want to know how you are going to perform on game day and what I can expect from you."*

He said it would cause quite a stir among the players as during the next couple of days they stopped to think about how they were going to do their best on game day. So when they came into his office he had moved all the furniture away from the center of the room and put two chairs face-to-face only five feet apart. He looked into each player's eyes with intensity and leaned forward to ask, *"What kind of performance can I count on you for game day?"* He said that the players were so "hyped" by the time that they got to sit nose-to-nose with him, they would discuss how they were going to play their very "<u>best</u>," make improvements, or how they would never let him down.

McCartney's response to them was, *"John, I am going to hold you to it. I am putting you on your 'honor' to deliver."* Many of these players would not even have an opportunity to play because there were more than 60 players on the team, but they were ready on game day. The intensity permeated the team. McCartney concludes that if you put a good man of character **<u>on his honor</u>** he will deliver.

CHARACTER QUALITY

- Put Your Talents to Work -

The door to opportunity is always labeled "push." While our Creator has given us uniqueness and an abundance of resources, He gave us talents, skills, intelligence, personality and physical strengths and He wants us to <u>aggressively</u> use them.. Like any investor, He wants to see our talents maximized by hard work using His principles for real riches.

Willie Gary and "Rudy" Ruettiger both have something in common. Willie went to college without a dime hoping to earn a football scholarship. He came from a family of sharecroppers. Willie's father taught him to "work for free" if that is what it takes to get ahead and he did. He impressed the football coach so much with his attitude that as a scholarship became available he was given one. Through Willie's hard work he became a lawyer and now is a judge in Florida.

Rudy's story has received national recognition on film. No matter how he was "put down" as too small and an underachiever, he lived out his dream with "heart." God believed in Rudy and his "never quit" attitude led him to Notre Dame to participate on the football practice squad. The movie portrays his work ethic and unwillingness to quit. He received his degree and now is a highly successful motivational speaker around the country.

Both men worked hard, built their character, and discovered their talents...their faith brought them through. God is calling us to work our mind, exercise our talents and plant the same. They're seed in the lives of other people.

Eagle Scout

At the age of 13, Sam Walton became an Eagle Scout...at the time the youngest boy in the history of the state of Missouri. Boy Scouts has been an organization through the years built on the whole concept of *"On my honor, I will..."* His mother motivated Sam by telling him to be the best that he could be in anything he undertook. His family struggled during the depression but he worked his way through college before working for the J. C. Penney Company. There he was impressed with the values established through the "Penney idea" before he had to enter military service. Even though he became "the wealthiest man in the world" through the growth and development of Wal-Mart, he never focused on money, material wealth or possessions. He was driven by the values of focusing on the customer, honesty, hard work and doing his best for his fellowman.

"Success is not about winning basketball games but about being faithful."
John Wooden

The Talent For Popcorn

Orville Redenbacher was raised on a farm in Indiana. Eating popcorn was a family tradition. As he grew up he had a burning passion to find a better quality popcorn with fewer wasted kernels. Through the years he would peddle his new popcorn on roadside stands and finally attempted to bring it into chain stores. When he reached a point of utter frustration, he stopped to think about the things that his mother had told him.

He shared in Guidepost, *"Talent, I thought about that for a long time — and what I had done with my abilities since I was a young man. Mom had talked about talents. When I practiced my coronet at home as a youngster she would wince at my bleeping."* She said, *"God gave you your share of talents, son, but playing the coronet is not one of them."* He continued, *"Yes, God had given me talents. I believed they were from Him. I even taught about talents as a Sunday School teacher. Sometimes the teaching tickled my memory about seeking advisors. I picked up my Bible and rifled through the pages. Yes, there it was...Proverbs 24:6 "For wise guidance you can wage your war, and in abundance of counselors there is victory.' (RSV)."*

Orville drew inspiration from the words and pulled together a team of friends as advisors who encouraged him to seek an advertising agency who came up with the theme, concept and packaging to create the "Orville Redenbacher Gourmet Popcorn" image. It was the turning point to create a business which set a new standard for the food industry.

"The best way to be successful is to follow the advice you give others."

FIRE AND PRESSURE

Fire destroys forests, while farmers use it to burn away old crops or mature sugar cane before harvest, yet fabricators use it to make glass or steel. Pressure in the earth over hundreds or thousands of years will form oil, ores, minerals and diamonds.

God uses the same principles sometimes in our lives to mold us, and build our character. You may think you are in the middle of a tragedy while it is a fire to burn away the old for a new crop to be planted in your life. At the same time the pressure may be so great you want to give up before your character and personality have matured to take on a whole new responsibility that you have never dreamed of.

Hold on tight and turn to God and in His time He will reveal the answers and the meaning to our agony. We have to take the first step. We can't see the future and we need to learn patience. It all becomes character building, part of his first laws.... "take on His image."

Wise Counsel

It is too bad Orville Redenbacher never knew Bob Nourse. Bob helped operate and close down his brother's business of many years and struggled for months about what he would do with his life. He saw his experiences as limited to the manufacturing business. But somehow he was fascinated with learning and growing and had a natural talent for facilitating and listening. He also had a compassion to help others grow and avoid mistakes.

During his struggles to find a new career at 52, he turned to God and went to church every day early in the morning saying, "*Oh, God, what am I going to do with my life?*" He told his wife that he dreamed he had "*a stainless steel tube through which God would send me messages.*" With the advice and encouragement of friends he went out one day in the country by himself to seek God's vision and develop a new plan for a business to help CEOs of companies.

That business today has hardly changed from the principles of Bob's vision. The business now operates worldwide and helps CEOs of noncompeting businesses in small groups which gather together one day a month to learn, grow, exchange and "sharpen their talents." The business is internationally known as The Executive Committee (TEC) and has over 5,000 CEOs and entrepreneurs internationally. It has been the standard bearer for a whole new service industry helping CEOs make better decisions and get ahead of the rapid growth of competition.

> *"Work harder on improving yourself,
> than your job."*
>
> **Jim Rohn**

The Woman of Inspiration

Mary Kay, founder of Mary Kay Cosmetics, a multi-billion dollar firm, says, "*When I meet someone, I imagine her wearing an invisible sign that says, 'Make me feel important!' This is one of the most important lessons in dealing with people I have ever learned.*

I believe that each of us has God-given talents within us waiting to be brought into fruition. Every person is unique and special. It doesn't matter what you do for a living or how much money you have in the bank, or how you look. People are people and everyone is important. I just try to look for the good qualities in everybody."

At appropriate times she shares her personal growth experience. Once when recovering from cancer chemotherapy treatment she shared, *"As the Apostle Paul tells us in the Bible, he had a thorn in the flesh. He prayed many times to God to remove that thorn, but for whatever reason, He didn't choose to do so. But Paul continued to serve the Lord. I visualize my cancer as my thorn in the flesh.*

In time I began to realize that God was using me to reach other women. They saw how I endured my illness with courage, grit, and determination. In spite of the chemo, I had a high level of energy. I can't begin to tell you how many women have said to me, 'I was feeling sorry for myself because of my personal troubles, but then I look at you and I realized I had nothing to complain about. If you can do what you have done, I can overcome my problems'."

> *"If our desires are to be the things of the world, they are never to be satisfied."*
> **Ben Franklin**

The Talent For Making Money

John D. Rockefeller's foundation has given over a billion dollars to various individuals and organizations for very significant causes. In his own mind John D. was a steward of God's will.

He said, *"I believe the power to make money is a gift from God — just as are the instincts for art, music, literature, the doctor's talent, and yours — to be developed and used to the best of our ability for the good of mankind. Having been endowed with the gift I possess, I believe it is my duty to make money and still more money and to use the money for the good of my fellowman according to the dictates of my conscience."*

> *"A man is rich according to what he* **is***, not according to what he* **has***."*

Service of the Master

The $3 billion public company with 200,000 employees, known as ServiceMaster, is a conglomerate of five different divisions serving hospitals, schools and homeowners. Their statement of business philosophy is:

>To honor God in all we do
>To help people develop
>To pursue excellence
>To grow profitably

Often ranked one of the most profitable, they consider their business concept of "stewardship" as the driving force of their business. James Heskett, a Harvard business school professor, has described ServiceMaster's approach as a "quality wheel" in which *"employee development and satisfaction lead to high motivation, which leads to a higher level of service quality, which leads to a great customer satisfaction, which leads to increased volume and increased rewards, which further fuels employee satisfaction and ability to develop new people."*

Bill Pollard, the current Chairman, says in his book, The Soul of the Firm, *"But profits for us is a means goal, not an end goal. What does it profit a man if he gains the whole world but loses his own soul? ...if we focus exclusively on profit, we would be a firm that had failed to nurture its soul. Eventually, I believe, firms that do this experience a loss in direction and purpose of their people, a loss in customers, and then a loss in profits.*

We make money at ServiceMaster. Our return on equity has averaged 50%. During the past twenty years, a share of our stock has grown in value from $1.00 per share to over $28.00 per share."

Sometimes the statement about God raises eyebrows, like this statement made by a shareholder, *"While I firmly support the right of an individual to his religious convictions and pursuits, I totally fail to appreciate the concept that ServiceMaster is, in fact, a vehicle for the work of God. The multiple references to this effect, in my opinion, do not belong in any annual business report. To interpret a service for profit (which is what ServiceMaster does) as the work of God is an incredible presumption. Furthermore, to make a profit is not a sin. I urge that next year's business report be confined to just that — business."*

Bill responded this way, *"I believe there is a link. Profit is a means in God's world to be used and invested, not an end to be worshipped. Profit is a legitimate measure of the value of our effort. It is an essential source of capital. It is a requirement for survival of the individual, the family unit, and any organization of society, whether it be a for profit company or not for profit organization. If you do not generate a surplus out of your annual operations, you will not generate a positive net worth. If you do not have a positive net worth, you will be operating in the red with a deficit. No organization, whether for profit or not for profit, can survive with continuing deficit."*

In discussing their personal influence on the employees, Pollard makes this statement: *"Some people may either question the existence of God or have different definitions for God. That is why at ServiceMaster we never allow religion or the lack thereof to become a basis for exclusion or how we treat each other professionally or personally. At the same time, I believe the work environment need not be emasculated to a neutrality of no belief."*

"The mighty oak was once a little nut that stood its ground."

The Game Plan

Joe Gibbs, former NFL Coach in the Hall of Fame, says, *"The Bible is our game plan by God for the world. The world says you've got to make money, gain position and win football games. God says that is not it at all. He says if you have the right perspective of all those things, God is the key on those things.*

The only way to please the world is to win every time. Just read the newspapers. But that is not God's way. He loves us more when we have tough times than when we are winning.

The world says you only live one life — so live it until you die. The Bible says no, that your soul and spirit will live forever. The question becomes where?"

The Telescope

Clint Purvis, Chaplain for the Florida State football team, says *"The Bible is a telescope...it brings God, His standards and our life into focus. But to first move the dial on the telescope requires a commitment to Him...a commitment to become spiritual and open to His leading. Our author of life wants men and women who sincerely seek Him. Otherwise, we can peer through the telescope to see a book that seems fuzzy, historical, dull and of little sense.*

The Bible is the key to spiritual growth. Just like our body needs food to grow or survive and the soul (or mind) needs an exchange of information to learn, the spirit needs the Word of God. Many times I feel the words penetrate my heart as I read His scripture."

ANYWAY

People are unreasonable, illogical, and self-centered,
Love them anyway.
If you do good, people will accuse you of ulterior motives,
Do good anyway.
If you are successful, you will win false friends
and true enemies,
Succeed anyway.
The good you do today, will be forgotten tomorrow,
Do good anyway.
Honest and frankness makes you vulnerable,
Be honest and frank anyway.
People favor underdogs, but follow only top dogs,
Fight for some underdogs anyway.
What you spend years building may be destroyed overnight,
Build anyway.
People really need help, but may attack you if you help them,
Help people anyway.
Give the world the best you've got,
you will get kicked in the teeth,
Give the world the best you've got anyway.

Dr. Robert Schuller

THE MORAL OF THE STORIES:

1. He is calling us to run our business and our life by His higher standards. The world's measure of success is touted as:

   (1) money, wealth and size

   (2) power and position

   (3) possessions

   (4) the social scene

   These are not God's priorities or ways of measuring us. His Book makes no promises of these things. His promises are spiritual leading to peace, joy and a sense of fulfillment. We can acquire some of the world's measure of success by His grace, inheritance, goals or circumstances and obeying His truths but by themselves they will not buy love, peace or spiritual things which are more lasting. Life is eternal. We come into this earthly life naked as a little child and leave the same way.

2. Paraphrasing the Bible, *"To whom much is given, much is required."* We are not all given the same talents or inheritance, but we are expected by God to maximize them, bringing a return on His investment in us. He loved us enough to bring us into the world and give us our talents. He is there to guide us and lead us all along the way, ready to give out many blessings. As one man put it, *"Do your best, God will do the rest."*

3. The things we earn by work and talent, and even those things we don't accomplish, are much more meaningful and cause us to grow closer to His image and purposes. Again, it is part of our character development.

4. He is working in our lives whether we recognize His hand or not. He will allow consequences and temptations of the world confuse, frustrate or lead us into temporary joy or frustration. He allows us to go from Chicago to Dallas to Miami to get to Milwaukee (two steps forward and one step back). He wants us to take the route that builds our character by His standard and which opens the door for eternal success.

5. "Missing the mark" — Many people live life just working their God-given talents and doing their best to be a "moral" person.

As a result, they may acquire money, possessions, respect and a good family but miss the real understanding of peace, love, joy and fulfillment with knowing Him in a spiritual relationship (Chapters 5-8).

> ### *What Do We Worship?*
>
> **Laziness** — *is the lack of motivation from little or no faith in oneself or the true God. While it can relate to physical energy, it has more to do with the "grip" on the heart than the body or soul. It is an avoidance of pain, avoiding the fear of failure while interacting with other people. Sleep, T.V., and food are ways to avoid reality and not have to deal with the fear inside. To God it is waste of talent and love.*

ONE NATION UNDER GOD

Creation Truth: *To rule over every living creature*

Character Quality: *Leading by example*

Saved By America

Frederick Phillips is the retired CEO of Phillips Electronics, a $45 billion Dutch company he founded along with his father. During World War II Frederick was put into concentration camp for nearly three years by the German Gestapo. His wartime experience and appreciation leads him to make a powerful statement about the United States. He says, *"America saved Europe four times. First, during World War I, then World War II, then with the Marshall Plan, and finally, saving us from nuclear destruction and the cold war."*

The First Freedom

President Ronald Reagan said, *"I believe this blessed land was set apart in a very special way, a country created by men and women who came here, not in search of gold, but in search of God. They would be free people, living under the law with faith in their Maker and their future."*

The pilgrims came to America to escape religious persecution of kings and monarchs in England and Holland. It was a turbulent time when kings thought nothing of enslaving or beheading people if they did not attend the church of state. Even the Pope thought during The Great

Crusade, there was nothing wrong with war and violence to acquire territories to spread or maintain his Christian gospel. The pilgrims were the first real settlers in America and their purpose was to seek religious freedom. It became America's cornerstone and inspiration for other freedoms to follow.

CHARACTER QUALITY

- Lead by example -

Abraham Lincoln, as a man of principles and character under great personal pressure, taxed his leadership ability to preserve our nation through the Civil War. The Battle of Gettysburg was a tragic time but his words will forever be remembered.

"Four score and seven years ago our fathers brought forth on this continent, a new nation, conceived in liberty, and dedicated to the proposition that all men are created equal."

He ended with these words, *"we here highly resolve that these dead shall have not died in vain—that this nation, under God, shall have a new birth of freedom—and that the government of the people, by the people, for the people, shall not perish from the earth."*

Before 1776, there were no democracies. America's principles of freedom have been an inspiration to nearly half of the world's nations who have replicated parts of our model, including England and recently former Communist countries.

It is self-evident that God has blessed America because of the faithfulness of its founders and believers. The key is whether other nations can grasp our spiritual and moral ethic, as well as our form of government.

Washington, The Man of Destiny

It may be rarely seen in history books but George Washington fought for the British long before the American Declaration of Independence. As an officer for the British he was involved in an ambush by a tribe of Indians. While a number of officers' lives were lost, somehow Washington retreated with a small group, barely escaping with their lives. As he returned to the fort he discovered there were four bullet holes in his coat, but no blood or injury to his body. Many called it a miracle, and years later George Washington had an opportunity to meet the Indian Chief who led the massacre. He personally told Washington that he had shot at him seventeen times and that he wanted to meet this man who seemed to be "invincible." George Washington was protected by God for a greater destiny.

In recognition of the Pilgrims, one of George Washington's early official acts as the first President of the United States was the proclamation establishing Thanksgiving as a holiday. He wrote, ***"Whereas it is the duty of all nations to acknowledge the providence of Almighty God, to obey His will, to be grateful for His benefits, and to humbly implore His protection and favor..."*** He went on later to call the nation to thankfulness for Almighty God.

The Conviction of Our Founders

Some of our skeptics and critics have wanted to disavow the research and proof that nearly all the founding fathers were Christians by their persuasion or convictions. They refer to them most notably as deists (a belief in God but also a belief that God would not interfere in the acts of men after his creation). One of these, Benjamin Franklin at 81 years of age during the Constitutional Convention made passioned efforts to get resolve on the differences and get beyond deadlocks that threatened the adoption of the Constitution. He said, *"The small progress we have made after four or five weeks is melancholy proof of the imperfections of the human understanding."*

He reminded the delegates that during the War for Independence they had prayed regularly to God in that very hall: *"Our prayers, sir, were heard, and they were graciously answered."*

Have we forgotten this powerful friend, or do we imagine that we no longer need His assistance? I have lived, sir, a long time, and the longer

I live, the more convincing proofs I see of this truth — that God governs in the affairs of men. And if a sparrow cannot fall to the ground without His notice, is it probable that an empire cannot rise without his aid? We have been assured, sir, in the sacred writings, that 'unless the Lord builds the house, its builders labor in vain.' I firmly believe this; and I also believe that without His concurring aid we shall succeed in this political building, no better than the builders of Babel." Franklin then suggested daily prayers, led by one of Philadelphia's clergymen.

A Nation of Morals and Virtue

John Adams, the second President of the United States and one of the outspoken founders, said in 1786, *"Our Constitution is wholly inadequate for any nation but a religious and moral nation."*

Pope John Paul II said in a recent visit to the United States, to heed America's founding fathers, *"Every generation of Americans needs to know that freedom consists not in doing what we like, but in having the right to do what we ought. Democracy needs virtue, if it is not to turn against everything it is meant to defend and encourage. Democracy stands and falls with the truths and values which it embodies and promotes."*

Alexis de Toqueville, the noted French political philosopher of the nineteenth century, visited America in her infancy to find the secret of her greatness. As he traveled from town to town, he talked with people and asked questions. He examined our young national government, our schools and centers of business, but could not find in them the reason for our strength. Not until he visited the churches of America and witnessed the pulpits of this land "aflame with righteousness" did he find the secret of our greatness. Returning to France, he summarized his findings: *"America is great because America is good; and if America ever ceases to be good, America will cease to be great."*

Individual and business freedom requires self-discipline and respect for others through the principles of morality.

Admitting The Obvious

Ted Koppel stated in a commencement speech given at Duke University, *"In place of truth, we have discovered facts. For moral absolutes, we have substituted moral ambiguity. We now communicate with everyone and say absolutely nothing. We have reconstructed the Tower of Babel, and it is a television antenna. There have always been imperfect role models, false gods of material success and shallow fame. But now their influence is magnified by television."* He also stated that it is *"The Ten Commandments, not the ten suggestions."*

Biblical Roots

The New England Primer was published for children in the early educational system by the colonists. It was a collection of Bible teachings pulled together in one book to teach reading. It had a great deal to do with teaching values and morals to young people for nearly a century, helping to build the American fiber.

The University of Houston's study on the Constitution found that 34% of the verbiage came from the Bible and as well the model for our court system. Wallbuilders, founded by David Barton of Aledo, Texas is dedicated to researching and sharing the principles and information upon which America was founded.

Inscribed on our money are the words, *"In God We Trust."* Similar quotes and Bible references are inscribed in or on the Capitol, Washington Monument, The Library of Congress, the Lincoln Memorial, Jefferson Memorial, and Dirkson Office Building. The Ten Commandments are inscribed above the head of the Chief Justice of the Supreme Court, and a prayer is said every day before sessions are begun in the House and Senate. There is little doubt that God has *"shed His grace on thee,"* even with all our failings and skeptics.

"He intervenes in the affairs of men by invitation only."

War, Prayer and Prosperity

World War II may have been the greatest time in the growth of America's character. Prayer was the key. Americans in the U.S. were praying for the soldiers abroad; the soldiers abroad were praying for their families at home and the war effort. Great sacrifices were made. Ethnic prejudices and national origins were set aside. America was brought closer together fighting enemies on both sides of the world with a national reliance on God.

Historians say the Normandy invasion could not have been accomplished without its surprised elements facilitated by the right weather (after it had been postponed two days) that produced a fog to cover the amphibious landing of troops that surprised the Germans. Eisenhower called it the Great Crusade and the code words for mission accomplished were *"Praise the Lord."*

The 1950's may have been the greatest time of prosperity and tranquility in America's history. Many say it was not because of our own great intelligence, might and determination but a loving God who blessed us for our faithful and righteous acts of sacrifice.

Americans remained in a "state of thanksgiving" after the war was over because their prayers had been answered. It was considered the greatest time of economic prosperity and tranquility in America. War, tragedy and catastrophe brings greater numbers to prayer than any other events.

There were other wars that had a significant impact on America's character and spirit, i.e., the Civil War and even the Civil Rights Movement. Amazingly, Sadam Hussein declared during the Gulf War that his god would lead him to victory over America. Even our news media was urging Americans to say a prayer for our soldiers. Unbeknownst to most of us, the military took 50,000 body bags to the Middle East in preparation for the worst. The casualties did not exceed 300. Was that because of our great military might, technology, planning and strategy? Faith says there was a higher power leading us to do what was right.

"America is God's second Noah's Ark"

Economic Leader

When examining world history, how could a nation in just 150 years become the greatest economic power the world has ever seen? Was it because we were smarter? Diverse people with great talent? Had more resources? Or a great educational system? Or was it because we had the right principles from founders who sought the right God using the right manual for success?

World Missions

The Bible says, *"Give and it is given unto you."* The tongue and cheek joke often quoted around the world is, *"If you want to build yourself into a great economic power, you should first have a war with the United States, lose, and they will give you all the money you need to start over and teach you how to do it."* In addition to the money our country gives to nations around the world, 90% of the world's mission giving for spreading the gospel comes from Americans.

Some might say, if the principles of a Judeo-Christian faith drive the system of America's economic might, then how can Japan become such a great economic success? Before World War II, Japan was ruled by military and a monarchy. The war humbled the Japanese; we trained them in the principles, *"Love your customers, employees, and neighbor as yourself,"*(Golden Rule), taught our ethics based on God's moral truths, limited their military, got them into the automobile industry, taught them quality, set up their government and free enterprise system, gave them the money and bought their products. Yes, the Japanese combined this with their intelligence, hard work and aggressiveness—all part of His truths.

Germany was also humbled and returned to its Christian heritage and principles and used our financial and management assistance to regain its strength by focusing on The Golden Rule.

"Our weakness becomes strength when we depend upon Him to carry the heavy end."

Four Significant Deterrents

Yet there is drawing away from Biblical truths in our society. There are a number of events and circumstances that have seriously detracted from America's resolve, convictions and principles, such as:

The 1963 decision by the Supreme Court to ban school prayer. Since that time serious violent crime has significantly increased 500%, divorces have more than doubled, values have deteriorated, SAT scores remain the same or declined.

With good intentions, many entitlement and welfare programs have deflated the human spirit of many of our citizens. Creativity and initiative are literally desensitized. People become controlled by a system, their freedoms are limited and they look to government for their answers, rather than turning to God, faith in themselves and self-determination to resolve their own needs.

False perceptions are created by the media and communication industry. Local reporters monitoring police reports emphasize crime over the good accomplished by 97% of the population. Crime is no longer "news." They create the image that morals are not important and have no bearing or consequences on society.

Finally, we have the increasing threat of too many lawyers (we have 70% of the world's lawyers and only 5% of the population) seeking cases and chasing high ticket judgments no matter what the scruples or integrity of their clients. Unfortunately some seek greed and power, rather than integrity. Their mission seems to be to find the loopholes in the law. As John Adams referred, the American Constitution was written for a nation of moral people, doing what is right.

THE MORAL OF THE STORIES:

1. America, with all its faults, is God's best hope and example for the world because of its founders and believers who today work toward modeling His character.
2. Myth: Separation of church and state is not part of our Constitution. Our fathers intended that the government would

not establish a single denomination as the official church of the government of the United States (as done in England). Their intent was to provide freedom of choice, not keep religious teaching out of government or schools.

3. For the hearts of people to be open to God, He wants nations where freedom and witness can exist without retribution. He is the founder of the principle of freedom. He gave each of us free will in life...the choice to believe or not believe. Many of His truths will work for the nonbeliever equally well as for the believer. He loves us all.

4. While surveys indicate that anywhere between 33-46% of Americans are committed Christians, are many of us blessed and protected because of their prayers? Or is it because of the commitment of our founding fathers and the generations of blessings God promises in scripture? Or both?

5. The secrets to continued economic success are dependent on the proper application of God's truths. America is more successful than other nations because it uses them more often. Yet, its potential is far from being realized.

6. The reason why eleven Presidents and Congresses since 1950 have so strongly defended the rights of Israel is not because the Israelis are always right but because He is working through the hearts of Americans to protect our Judeo-Christian heritage for a greater plan yet to come.

7. Why have SAT scores and so many other negative consequences occurred since the 1963 act by the Supreme Court of removing prayer from school? When we fail to respect and live by His truths, the consequences are negative in the long term.

8. The Spirit of our founders and the laws they established were to give new individual and corporate freedoms never before granted in the world. Our freedoms required moral people who believed in a higher power and seek Him, not big government, for their needs.

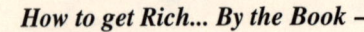

SPIRITUAL TRUTHS

The inner core of every human being is a spirit... often referred to as the "heart." God is **The Spirit of love, truth and light** who communicates with our inner spirit, dependent on our relationship with Him.

The first four commandments of the Ten Commandments call us to be open to His leading. When Jesus was asked what is the greatest commandment of all, He said first, *"Love your Lord God with all your heart, soul and might. . ."* summarizing these four commands in one phrase.

He wants a personal relationship with each of us, to love us daily. He created us to never be alone. He wants us to learn His ways and grow closer to the purposes He has for each of us... as we do, His leading and involvement becomes apparent... without it we may miss His guiding.

Through visions and insight, He inspires many to start, grow or turnaround businesses.

True peace, love and joy can only be found through our spiritual and serving relationship with Him... **this is the secret to real riches in life.**

How to get Rich... By the Book

The last six truths of the Ten Commandments are guidelines for loving our fellowman. The Lord embodied them when He said to "Love your neighbor as yourself.". Also known as the golden rule is "Do unto others as you would have them do unto you."

These truths have become the most widely accepted foundations for business ethics in America with growing acceptance throughout the world.

As businesses and individuals continue to learn ways to love (care, empathy, listening and servicing their needs), their neighbor (employees, customers, suppliers, vendors, community and stockholders)...plus using their God given talents by His will, they shall become more richly blessed.

Being "customer focused" was His design long before the CEOs, business authors, consultants and professors discovered it as the central way to succeed in business.

THE MEEK SHALL INHERIT

Spiritual Truth: *Have no other Gods before Me.*

Character Quality: *By being humble and trusting Me.*

The Core of the Problem

Coach Bill McCartney describes an incident which can be exemplary of our problem. He had just walked on to the practice field with his players and not 30 minutes later his trainer called across the field and said, *"Coach, there is a phone call for you."* McCartney yelled back, *"You know I don't take phone calls during practice."* And the trainer yelled back, *"Yea, Coach, but its <u>Sports Illustrated</u> calling."* McCartney thought for a moment or two and finally said, *"Okay, I will be there, have him hang on."*

He had to walk all the way across three practice fields, up a large ramp to his office in the stadium. As he walked he started thinking about *"What do they want from me? Perhaps they want to write an article to set the records straight about some of the awful things they said about us last year when we won the national championship. Or perhaps they want to write about how we should really be ranked no. 1 over two other contenders in the polls."*

As he mulled over in his mind how he would answer these questions, he finally got to his office and picked up the phone. He said hello and the person on the other end said, *"Hello, Mr. McCartney?"* He said, *"Yes."* *"This is Sports Illustrated and we needed to call you because your subscription is about to run out."* As McCartney shares that story, he says it is typical of how self-centered we can become and how we can place higher importance on ourselves than we deserve.

CHARACTER QUALITY

- Be humble and trust Me -

Dr. Laura Nash, author of the book, <u>Believers in Business</u>, says that through her interviews with Christian CEOs she learned that "the problem with ego is not with having an ego but with losing one's proper perspective. The problem can be expressed in quantitative terms of excess - thinking too much of one's own ability — or it can be expressed in terms of relationships. Hyperinflated self-regard contributes to a broken relationship with God and with one's neighbor."

Dean Sherman asks the question, "Are you a horse, mule or sheep?" Sometimes to get the attention of a horse you have to slap him up side the head, and with a mule it is typical to use a 2 x 4, but with a sheep comes a good follower. The Lord does not want us to lose our aggressiveness or willingness to take risks, but He also wants us to be as meek as sheep to listen and be used by Him and our fellowman. The plan is for us to be servant and not king.

Being our Creator, omnipotent and invisible, allows Him to work through us in ways that we can't totally fathom. Two things bother Him significantly...arrogance and ignorance, yet He is incredibly tolerant with us for long periods of time.

As the first commandment, having no other Gods becomes our most pivotal choice and affects every other relationship and attitude throughout our entire life.

The question is whether we are so "prideful" in our own success or accomplishments that we don't need any other God besides ourself— we are in total control and fear losing it. Life's character lessons sometimes get our attention, if we just allow ourselves to be humble and trust Him.

"Most people wish to serve God... But only in an advisory capacity."

Never Quit

Many would call John Scott a self-made man. By the time he was 28 years old he had a retail chain of eight stores and was already a millionaire. But then he encountered some up and down experiences that caused him to revert back to his college athletic career and the attitude of "never, never quit." After he built the business up to 28 different locations, some of his products started to become "commodities" as they were introduced through the discount stores of Wal-Mart and K-Mart. He had to start cutting back and looking for other sources of capital to rebuild. His corporate and personal debt were escalating.

A couple of competitors offered to buy his chain but he declined. After reducing to 12 stores he was offered $5 million. At 6 stores he was offered $3 million, and finally the last offer was $1 million before he was forced to close and liquidate whatever assets remained. John considered himself a Christian and claimed to pray for God's direction. Most of his advisors urged him to sell and get out at each of the stages, but he confused selling with quitting. It is hard for many people to become meek enough to listen and stop being too proud to be "right."

"Many CEOs go broke because they won't subject their ideas for possible criticism."
Brian Tracey

Being Open

In the late 1960's, Charles Smith was forced to take over as CEO of a struggling $30 million company but through his determination, financial savvy and openness, he parlayed the company into a $2 billion conglomerate. With national publicity and recognition, he was considered a highly respected and sought after CEO. He was befriended by another corporate head who had his own $2 billion company but was seeking to retire and phase out. He persuaded Charles to buy his personal stock and come on his board as he transitioned out.

Charles was advised by friends and business associates not to buy, but he had gone through twelve years of 47% compounded growth and saw great potential in this corporation. He had stopped listening and felt invincible. Unfortunately what he had not visualized was a coming recession and that his friend had not laid out all the facts nor been totally open and honest with him. Within a year Charles was forced to take over as CEO and turn the company around. Results were disastrous for the company he built as well as for the company he acquired.

Today he wishes he had listened to those who were giving him wise counsel. His personal assets went from $60 million to $10 million...the big lesson learned.

"Don't trust yourself to be your own god."

The Control Factor

Of all the ways we become deceived, the most critical is our fixation with looking good...we believe we have to be in control. It's an attitude that we "don't want to look stupid" in the eyes of other people, which is perpetuated throughout our society.

The bottom line is that there is only one person in control...the one who created us. No matter what we think we have done on our own, He has been available to help...depending on His purpose and plan.

We can work with Him or against Him...life is just much more peaceful and rich if we surrender to His control.

The Invincible Giant

IBM for years has been considered to be the No.1 Blue Chip company in the United States. They seem to have set the tone for professionalism, management, training and credibility. Unfortunately, the egotism and pride of the key executives impaired their vision and listening skills. The company that refused to ever lay anyone off went from 420,000 employees down to 200,000.

The customer was telling the corporate giant that the market was moving away from main frame computers to the personal (PC) computers for everyday use in most businesses. They passed up early opportunities to be the dominant leader in that segment as well as the software industry. Unfortunately many of the top executives had been entrenched in the "Big Blue" corporate pride, high salaries and bureaucracy, unable to listen and change with the marketplace.

IBM is rebounding with new and fresh outside leadership, maybe they will be humble enough to listen.

"He wants men great enough to be small enough to be used."

Egotism

Tom Phillips, former chairman of Raytheon, says that ego is the number one cause of business mistakes. For example, he relates, *"In most take over situations, the CEO goes to his board initially with incomplete information—by necessity. They recommend an offer, and only then are all the financials available. At that point it is almost impossible for a CEO to change his recommendation. His ego is on the line. It was his project. And yet that is precisely the point when a good leader must have the ability to say, 'that is not such a good deal after all'."*

My number one job is to please God."
Bobby Bowden

Wisdom

> God seeks humble, obedient listeners and followers and people led by His Spirit to unfold His plans. Evidenced by many Christians when asked to commit something may say, "Let me pray about it" to seek His confirmation.
>
> If we will not be humble before God, our missing Him eventually takes its toll and we become humble.

Getting "Buy In"

Richard Hagberg, the noted California consultant who specializes in working with high growth firms in the Silicon Valley, says that *"Typically CEOs are good at developing a vision, think they have communicated, but frequently their strategy is not widely understood. Their impatience drives them to focus on financial goals, which means they fail to build relationships with boards or their employees.*

When CEOs lose touch with their employees and they become isolated, they think they have 'buy in' but what they have is false consensus. They are far less effective in facilitating team work and gainful participation than they are in decision making.

If they see themselves as too self-important, they will be defensive because they have a vested interest in maintaining an image of themselves as omnipotent. And that can be an absolute killer."

> *"You should never let adversity get you down...*
> *Except on your knees."*

God Inspired

During the middle of the gas crisis in the early 1980's, a humble businessman by the name of Bob Harrison believed that God was leading him to buy a Chrysler dealership. It seemed crazy and illogical to him. People were turning in their gas guzzling cars as fast as they could and Chrysler was in a tailspin and had run out of capital. But he confirmed the leading of his heart with wise business counsel and bought a Southern

California dealership for less than $100,000 down. Within two years it was one of the top dealerships in Southern California. Years later Bob and his family sold the dealership and moved on to teach other businessmen about the Biblical concepts that he learned in being humble and listening to his God.

> *"Egotism is the only disease known to man that seems to make everybody sick... except the carrier."*
>
> **Charles "Red" Scott**

Hurricane Faith

Starting as the secretary to the President of Southeastern Metals fresh out of school was a traumatic experience for a young Nadine Gramling. But she learned quickly and became the Sales Manager and then the President, taking the company from $10 million in sales to $90 million.

She always shared her faith with her employees and through "her walk," but one day her faith was severely tested. After Hurricane Andrew, South Florida officials did a reassessment of their construction codes and "investigative reporters" singled out her company as being under standard.

For nearly four weeks the media was "in her face" in preparation for the county's testing of her metal roofing products. The danger was that if they failed the test, the company could be open for lawsuites and her distributors would drop their products. She said, *"We could have lost the whole company. I was not in control. I was involved in a circumstance I had never been prepared to face before. I turned to God and never prayed so hard in my entire life."*

The outdoor test was with a 2x4 shot twice from a cannon. It rained and the wood was twice as heavy as normal, leaving the margin of error only 1/16 of an inch. But by this time, she had received real peace of mind.

She concluded, *"We passed with flying colors only because of the grace of God. We were put under unfair circumstances and conditions. Only God could have pulled us through. He made the difference."*

> *"People with humility don't think less of
> themselves, they just think of themselves less."*
> **Ken Blanchard**

Kitchen Table Shoemaker

In the mid 1950's Bob Bowerman was a track coach at the University of Oregon constantly frustrated with the injuries of his athletes. He attributed many of the problems to the shoes typically sold to track athletes. So he began work on different ideas and concepts, at his kitchen table until he designed a new shoe that would be lighter, more comfortable and flexible. He tried to sell his concept to companies without success. Eventually he became totally discouraged.

One day in attempting to encourage his team he quoted the apostle Paul: *"Do you not know that in a race all the runners run, but only one gets the prize? Run in such a way as to get the prize."* (I Corinthians 9:24). He explained that winning is important, but not the only goal. Later he realized that very same advice applied to his life. It was as if God was saying to keep on running, to persevere, and that somehow he would get those shoes made, even if he had to do it himself.

So he hand-crafted a pair of shoes on his kitchen table and asked some of his runners to try them out. Their response was very encouraging. His miler, Phil Knight, became very enthusiastic about the shoes. After graduating from Stanford, Phil found the shoe manufacturers, distributors and developed a unique marketing concept. Little did Bob or Phil know that they were creating a whole new industry. They picked the name "Nike" for their company. The rest is history.

> *"God opposes the proud but gives
> grace to the humble."*
> **1 Peter 5:5**

The Meek Shall Inherit

Listening For A Small Voice

James Kraft, the founder of Kraft Foods peddled his cheese on a horse drawn wagon during the early days. At one point, he became very discouraged because sales were poor and his capital was exhausted. He saw himself as a failure.

One day he just stopped in total despair. He said, *"For the moment my mind was clear of frantic planning and thinking. It was a receptive interlude. And at that moment it came to me, clearly and distinctly, this conviction: 'You have been working without God'."*

I stopped to listen. For the first time in my life I had been able to hear the words which must have been spoken to the deaf ears of all of us over and over again. I resolved to let God have direction in my life. And from that moment forward, my life began to change in every way. Defeat was impossible — because I had been given an 'invincible asset.' I have never stopped listening since."

James Kraft's business became a phenomenal success, and he became a great spokesman for the power of God working in one's life. He said, *"In the stillness of spirit, a man is of listening heart and mind. He is conditioned spiritually for divine guidance. The second, and most direct route to inspiration, is the daily systematic habit of reading the Word of God, it speaks directly to men and women — powerfully, and personally. Daily reading the Bible, I am convinced, prepares the man and the heart for hearing the will of God.*

The third and safest, surest and swiftest road to victory is prayer — the habit of prayer which was once the familiar, everyday blessing that it was intended to be in this nation. Personal and family prayer, practiced daily in quietness of spirit, could, I believe, alter the whole world, as I know it alters individual lives."

> *"The main requirements of leadership are guts and judgment. To win trust you have to make yourself vulnerable."*
> **Michael H. Walsh**

The Wisdom of The Babe

During the last week of his life, Babe Ruth shared with Guidepost the following: *"As I look back now, I realize that the knowledge of our Creator was a big crossroads with me. I got one thing straight (and I wish all kids did) - that He is boss. He was not only my boss but boss of all my bosses. Up until then, like all bad kids, I hated most of the people who had control over me and could punish me. I began to see that I had a higher person to reckon with who never changed, whereas my earthly authorities changed from year to year. I finally realized that He was not only just, but merciful."*

THE MORAL OF THE STORIES:

1. "Have no other Gods before me" is about being teachable, open, listening, seeking, humbleness and trusting Him. He can speak to our heart directly, use other people, create or allow circumstances which ultimately get our attention. Those with wisdom seek Him.

2. Success or even inheritance in one's life can lead to a false confidence, pride, or even egotism. It is the self-made man or woman attitude ("I am my own man") that will not hold up for a lifetime let alone eternity. We either choose to be humble before God or He allows the weight of our own arrogance to create pain which will lead to humbleness.

3. The greatest intimidation for too many is that we will lose control or "look stupid" in the eyes of other people. That is why it is important to trust God because there is no way humanly possible for us to live a full, peaceful and joyous life with this anguish looming over us. No matter what we do, there will be times we lose control and look stupid, but it's okay, we can be forgiven.

4. He wants to be the God of everyday, not the God of last resort. He wants a personal daily relationship where we walk and talk together and He has an opportunity to love us as He intended and for us to love Him in return.

5. He created us and knows us intimately and our every need. But He wants to be asked to enter our life and lead us to greater success.

6. Yes, you need to be concerned about yourself with good planning, initiative, follow through, confidence, but not to the point of worry. Once you become so self-centered, you worry about yourself. He wants us to be God-centered and centered toward the interests of our fellowman.

7. The vision for truly, long-term successful businesses and organizations always comes from God working through people who are humble enough to receive the <u>vision</u> he puts on their heart.

What Do We Worship?

Pride/Egotism — *is a belief in one's self to the point of whatever I earn I get, I'm number one, the self-made man/woman, you can be anything you want to be, I am woman, I am strong, I control my own destiny, I am my own man, and I did it my way. Being proud of your family, business and friends is fine. Being proud without recognizing God and His blessings upon you shows "a lack of knowledge." He created each of us. So if we only use our God-given talents to get ahead or to become successful without sincerely thanking Him for those talents, we are blinded by deceit. We have, in effect, chosen to say, "I'm my own god." Typically we are self-centered, concerned about being right (having all the right answers), wanting always to be in control, or "looking good," and get defensive, when challenged and someone defies us, wanting to prove ourself right...all characteristics of pride gone too far. It is either arrogance or ignorance apart from God.*

What is Being Saved? (The Eternal Aspects of Success)

It is a state of grace and forgiveness that He freely gives us, when we sincerely ask. He is holy, and we are not, because of a world off course from His intent. He seeks a personal relationship that allows Him to cleanse our spirit, and live through us and assure us a place in Heaven.

We are saved from the lies, mistakes, pressures and lack of understanding that missing the mark (sin) tries to grip us with. We enter a state of grace that opens the door to a more fulfilling and loving life. Do we sin again? Probably, but as we seek His forgiveness, it is forgotten. Being saved is the beginning of an eternal journey that leads to His plan for our success.

The Meek Shall Inherit

Movement To And From His Truths

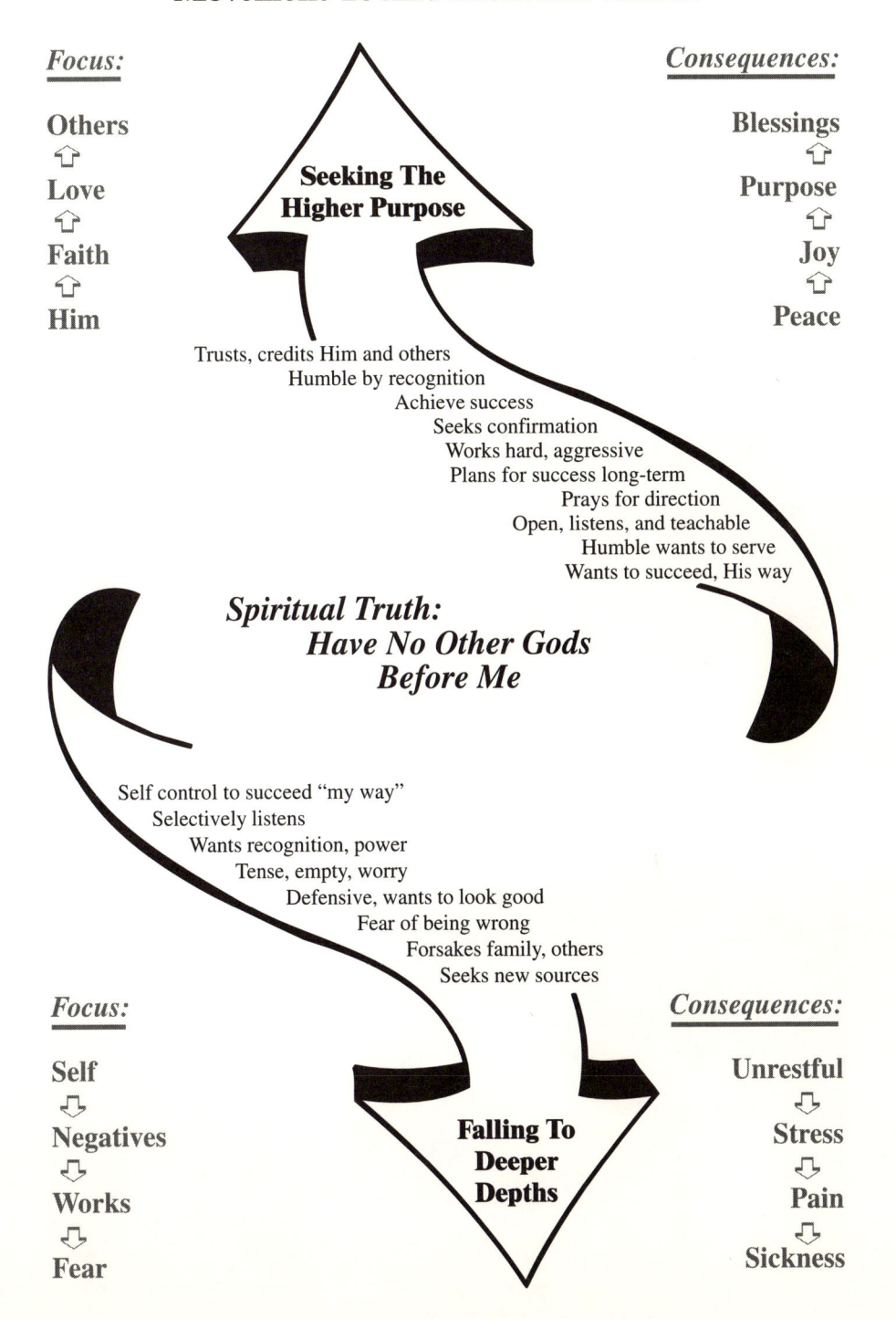

Focus:

Others
⇧
Love
⇧
Faith
⇧
Him

Seeking The Higher Purpose

Consequences:

Blessings
⇧
Purpose
⇧
Joy
⇧
Peace

Trusts, credits Him and others
Humble by recognition
Achieve success
Seeks confirmation
Works hard, aggressive
Plans for success long-term
Prays for direction
Open, listens, and teachable
Humble wants to serve
Wants to succeed, His way

Spiritual Truth:
Have No Other Gods
Before Me

Self control to succeed "my way"
Selectively listens
Wants recognition, power
Tense, empty, worry
Defensive, wants to look good
Fear of being wrong
Forsakes family, others
Seeks new sources

Focus:

Self
⇩
Negatives
⇩
Works
⇩
Fear

Falling To Deeper Depths

Consequences:

Unrestful
⇩
Stress
⇩
Pain
⇩
Sickness

6

FAILURE LEADS TO SUCCESS

Spiritual Truth: *Have no false idols*

Character Quality: *By being convicted and forgiven*

Heartbreak Can Open New Doors

Mary Kay worked eleven years for a national direct sales company as the national training director. With 1,500 women to oversee throughout the country, she was constantly traveling. Company sales were flat and turnover was high. She urged the top executive to give her help to be able to cover more territory and give the sales people the tools and encouragement in order to increase sales and profits. Her constant urgings fell on deaf ears.

Finally the Chief Executive decided to hire an assistant that Mary Kay would train. Elated, she did her best to coach and train the man. It allowed her to cut down on her travel and be involved in other aspects of increasing sales.

Within a year the Chief Executive promoted this new individual over her to national sales manager at twice the salary, a position she was already performing without the title. When she heard the news she went home and cried her heart out. She wrote a letter of resignation and never heard from the company again.

Little did this company know that Mary Kay was a woman of destiny and that God had a greater plan. She made no efforts to file a discrimination case but decided that she was going to encourage other women to get involved in the business world. She would write a book but as she laid out the qualities of her "dream company," she felt so convicted that she was being called to ...build a company that represents the ideals and principles that she believed and shared with others. Today her company approaches nearly $2 billion in sales with over 400,000 distributors.

> *"Experience is what you get when you don't get what you want."*

Conviction Overcomes Defeat

Few great leaders encounter defeat so consistently before enjoying ultimate victory as did this individual. A frequently reported listing of these failures include the following:

- Failed in business in 1831.
- Ran for the legislature and lost in 1832.
- Failed once in business in 1834.
- Sweetheart died in 1835.
- Had a nervous breakdown in 1836.
- Lost a second political race in 1838.
- Defeated for Congress in 1843.
- Defeated for Congress in 1846.
- Defeated for Congress in 1848.
- Defeated for the Senate in 1855.
- Defeated for Vice-President in 1856.
- Defeated for the Senate in 1858.

The man was Abraham Lincoln, elected 16th President of the United States in 1860.

> *"Success is never permanent, failure is never fatal."*

Failure Leads To Success

CHARACTER QUALITY

- Be Convicted and Forgiven -

As long as man and woman have existed on earth they have sought a god to worship. In the days of the Old Testament many created statues, golden calves, Buddha, while others worshipped the sun, the wind and/or the earth and called them gods.

In the American society, founded on Christian Biblical principles, we have experienced the greatest prosperity in the shortest period of time of any other nation on earth. So many of us are:

1. Too intelligent to fall for a "story of a savior dying on a cross."
2. Too complacent, prosperous or satisfied to care (believing that this is the way the good life is supposed to be).
3. Too hopelessly lost to understand.

Most of us have picked or chosen a variety of ***false idols*** to worship to fill the spiritual void in our lives. The Bible refers to these in different passages and they are most often recognized as the "Seven Sins of the Heart," caused from habits, bondage, inheritance or curse. They are pride/egotism, laziness, envy, greed, addictions, anger and lust. These false idols create a situation of trying to serve two masters. God knew it wouldn't work and that is why He told us to only worship Him.

Some people have to be fired, others end up in a hospital or lose a loved one before their "wake-up" call creates the humbleness and conviction He is waiting to see. He is ready to forgive us and love us, if we just have the faith to seek Him.

Failure can be a real "God-sent" experience that has a meaningful purpose for our lives.

A Second Chance

Alfred Nobel was a Swedish chemist who had great success in developing explosives used in a number of wars. He had become wealthy from his success. One day his brother passed away and the local newspaper wrote an obituary mistaking Alfred for his brother. The obituary described Alfred as a man who became rich by enabling people to kill each other in unprecedented numbers. Shaken by this assessment, Nobel resolved to use his fortune to honor the accomplishments of humanity rather than through destruction. He then created the Nobel Peace Prize, which recognizes several men and women throughout the world each year for their peaceful contributions to mankind.

> *"The way to succeed is to double your failure rate."*
> **Thomas J. Watson**

Open Book Management

Jack Stack, CEO of Springfield Remanufacturing Corporation ($200 million in sales) and author of the book, <u>The Great Game of Business</u>, by necessity forged a new business concept known as "Open Book Management" which many companies are attempting to grasp and implement today. But Jack's early life was a series of failures. As a child, he was such a problem his father was convinced that becoming a priest would change him. After being kicked out of seminary, his father tried reform school. After being kicked out again, Jack was convinced that going into the military would please his father. He was rejected by the military for physical reasons. He finally got a job sweeping floors for his father's company.

By attending night school, he eventually graduated from college and worked his way up the corporate ladder to become the plant manager of a division of International Harvester in Springfield, Missouri. In the midst of International Harvester's decline, Jack and other key executives wanted to "save their jobs" and proceeded to go to 54 banks before they finally arranged the financing to buy their division through one of the highest leveraged buy-outs in history ($100,000 down for a $9 million loan). Jack kept his faith and learned through each rejection. Today his business is considered one of the most innovative companies in America.

Pat Kelly, CEO of Physician Sales and Service, was raised in an orphanage and only saw his father twice after age six. His firing by a firm in Houston led him to start a new business with two partners that today represents one of the fastest growing companies in the United States with sales of $700 million in just 14 years.

Neither of these men were educated at Harvard. Their failures created humility and openness. Their convictions, determination and unique insights in business led them to further define "Open Book Management" which more closely aligns with principles of God's Moral Truths, further discussed in Chapter 10.

Open to the Vision

Ray Kroc, in his early years, dropped out of high school to play the piano in nightclubs and sell paper cups for a living. He even unsuccessfully tried his hand at investing in Florida real estate. After serving in the war, he came home and acquired the national marketing rights for multi-mixers to make milk shakes. As America moved into the suburbs in the 1950's, his business was failing.

He had heard of the McDonald brothers in San Bernardino, California, who sold 20,000 shakes a month using his equipment. The McDonald brothers had dropped their "car hops" to become the truly first "fast-food," self-serve restaurant with no frills. Their success had received some national attention and they had tried to franchise the concept, but with no success.

Ray Kroc visited their operation with the intent of encouraging them to expand so he could sell them more mixers. He spent all morning observing their operation from the parking lot. Mobs of people stood in line at lunch time to buy the 15 cent hamburgers, 10 cent fries and 15 cent shakes. After the crowd cleared, he introduced himself to the brothers and said, "My God, I've been standing out there looking at it but I could not believe it. I've got to become involved in this."

He encouraged them to find a new franchising agent to open more locations. But frankly they didn't want the travel or headaches. So only a few weeks later he called back to see whether they had found a new agent. When they said "no," he said he wanted to be that agent. The rest is history, even though he eventually gave up on his mixer business.

Ray Kroc said "It was life or death for me." He became humble and open enough to allow God to place a vision on his heart that has become the model for business success and franchising worldwide. Walt Disney also went through a personal financial crisis before he finally started calling his mouse "Mickey." Colonel Sanders was living in near poverty until he started to sell his special recipe for Kentucky Fried Chicken.

Failure breaks our pride and allows us to become humble enough for our spirit to listen to Him and receive a new direction in our lives.

"Human beings, like chickens, thrive best when they have to scratch for what they get."

There is a Purpose

Bobby Bowden, head football coach at Florida State University, says, *"There are two things that happened to me that shaped my career. When they happened I thought they were the worst things that ever happened to me. The first was when I was 13 years old. I was raised in a house that backed up to the high school football field. I could always hear the ball being kicked. That year I was hit with a disease that kept me in bed all year long. I thought that it was the worst thing that could have happened to me.*

My doctor had told me I would never play again. One day, my mom said to me, 'Bobby, do you believe in prayer?' I said, 'Yes, ma'am.' She said, 'Why don't you ask God to heal you?' I did and He did. That year in bed I learned to develop faith. It changed my life.

The second thing was when I was a junior in high school in Birmingham. In practice I broke my thumb. I continued to play but it got worse and worse. One day after school, I went to the doctor and he put it in a cast and my season was over. My coach said, 'Maybe I can get you another year of eligibility if you drop out of school now and we might get you a college scholarship.' My mom and dad agreed and I worked at home that year and gained 20 pounds (to 150) and got a scholarship. God used those experiences to develop my character, attitude, and faith and shaped the way I would go."

Wake-Up Calls

Here are some examples of some "wake-up calls" which should cause us to turn to God and look for spiritual direction in our seeking His love.

BUSINESS	PERSONAL
Losing money	Fight with your spouse
Poor performance review	Harm to a spouse or child
No raise	Feeling of emptiness
Being let go	Tension
Passed over for promotion	Death in the family
Boss is hard to work with	Fear of negatives
Company closes	Divorce
Verbal attacks by others	Economic pressures
Losing your temper	Relocation
Jealousy and hate	Added responsibilities
Violence	Addictions

The world is full of the tensions and problems that can create these circumstances, particularly if He is not protecting us. If we continue in the negatives, we have missed one or more of His truths. There are consequences for our actions. They may not be as immediate as we might expect, but in God's timing and mercy He can use these experiences...waiting for us to call on His name.

"God seldom picks the most qualified or best educated but the humble ...that is open, teachable and willing to serve."

The Right God

The late Pete Maravich, a great basketball star, said, *"I didn't want a crutch. I saw Christianity in just that way. My God was basketball. I had power, fame, 60 records, and my own Lear jet. I did 'show time' for thousands of people. Yet I was an alcoholic and into cults. I had everything that a 'successful' person supposedly wanted.*

Then one night I went to bed and I couldn't sleep. Every sin in my life came up. At 6:00 in the morning an angel said to me, 'be strong in Him in thine own heart, God still loves you, you can still come home.' My life has not been the same since."

> *"Don't be afraid of pressure. Remember that pressure is what turns a lump of coal into a diamond."*

The Gift of Watergate

Chuck Colson, former chief counsel to President Nixon, says, *"Life is a paradox. I thank God for Watergate because I learned the greatest lessons of my life. The teachings of Jesus are true. He who seeks to save his life will lose it, he who loses his life for My sake will find it."*

At 39 I was a successful attorney and asked to join the White House as Special Counsel to President Nixon. I had achieved what my dad told me was true: If you just work hard, put your mind to something, and go for it you can be successful, like the American dream. This became real in all the ego trappings that were there...limousines, servants and people gloating over you.

It was in prison when I really came to know the Lord and His peace — real meaning, real identity, real purpose and real security. The statements of two men really influenced my thinking: Alexander Solzhenitsyn, the Russian professor and philosopher, said while in prison, 'Bless you, bless you prison for being in my life because it is there laying on the prison straw and rotting that I realized that the purpose of life is not prosperity as we have been led to believe but the maturing of the soul'."

Failure Leads To Success

The second statement was by Blaise Pascal, the inventor of the computer, who said, *"There is a hole in our lives we try to fill with money, power, sex, drugs, work, recreation or any false idol that gets hold of our soul."*

"No Jesus, No Peace --Know Jesus, Know Peace"

The Grace Period

The three basic types of judgment are:
- *a) Justice - being convicted of a crime and receiving the full penalty you deserve;*
- *b) Mercy - being given a lesser punishment for your offense;*
- *c) Grace - someone else accepting the punishment for you.*

In God's design, Jesus paid the price for us but we must accept His grace on our behalf.

The term "grace period" came from God's allowance of a reasonable time to accept Him or taking action for the atonement of our mistakes (missing the mark). We may not see or sense the consequences because of God's grace for a long period. Sometimes he's waiting and hoping for repentance.

So the grace period is time between our mistake and our day of accountability, here or before Him.

Being Carried

President Ronald Reagan, addressing the National Prayer Breakfast in Washington in 1982, offered these remarks:

"Those of you who were here last year might remember that I shared a story by an unknown author, a story of a dream he had had. He had dreamt that he walked down the beach beside the Lord. And as they walked, above him in the sky was reflected each experience of his life.

And then reaching the end of the beach, he looked back and saw the two sets of footprints extending down the way, but suddenly noticed that every once in a while there was only one set of footprints. And each time, they were opposite a reflection in the sky of a time of great trial and suffering in his life. And he turned to the Lord in surprise and said, 'You promised that if I walked with You, You would always be by my side. Why did You desert me in my times of need?' And the Lord said, 'My beloved child, I wouldn't desert you when you needed Me. When you see only one set of footprints, it was then that I carried you.'

Well, when I told that story last year, I said I knew, having only been here in this position for a few weeks, that there would be many times for me in the days ahead when there would be only one set of footprints and I would need to be carried, and if I didn't believe that I would be, I wouldn't have the courage to do what I am doing.

Shortly thereafter, there came a moment when, without doubt, I was carried. (Later he referred to recovering from the bullet he took in the assassination attempt). *Well, God is with us. We need only to believe. The psalmist says, 'Weeping may endure for a night, but joy cometh in the morning.'*

Speaking for Nancy and myself, we thank you for your faith and for all your prayers on our behalf. And it is true that you can sense and feel that power.

I've always believed that we were, each of us, put here for a reason, that there is a plan, somehow a divine plan for all of us. I know now that whatever days are left to me belong to Him."

THE MORAL OF THE STORIES:

1. As we worship self-centered false idols of goals, activities or habits, we get entrapped in a "catch 22" which we struggle to break. Yet, struggles can be the things that God uses to fashion us for bigger and better things. Struggles can lead to "wake-up calls" which get our attention, get us refocused to seek Him. He allows our mistakes and failures to continually build our character.

2. If we won't listen and be humble, God will allow circumstances to convict us, mature us and get our attention.

3. During Old Testament times many people sought false gods through statues or idols. Today those false idols are more commonly termed The Seven Sins of the Heart. (Note: What Do We Worship in appendix in back of the book).

4. God loves each of us the same whether we are committed to Him or not. For example, Jim Bakker, the television evangelist of the 1980's, got caught in some of the same traps of pride, lust and greed as nonbelievers. He was trying to serve two gods, himself with his human desires and the one true God. Having two masters never works. God is jealous and eventually we trip ourselves.

5. Jamie Colter, the CEO of Lone Star Steakhouse and Restaurant, makes the statement, *"The biggest predictor of future failure is your current success."* We can individually or corporately be riding an incredible wave of "success." It is like we can't make a mistake. Climbing the ladder of success or growth in economic terms seems to cover a lot of the barnacles that we gather as we go through life looking at the short term or chasing what the world calls success. If the motives are wrong, failure or defeat will eventually catch up with us.

6. Experience can be one of the best or worst teachers. If your family, friends or even business has been teaching the wrong principles: pride/egotism, lust, addictions, laziness, envy, anger or greed; There is only one master "true" to serve, the one who created us. The world is full of deceit and false idols.

7. Many relate or find comfort in leaders, athletes, movie stars or media personalities. They can be good heroes if they know and respect the truth. Unfortunately, when they are deceived and self-centered, they become bad examples that many unknowledgeable or arrogant people find comfort in relating to as "If they can do it, it's okay, so can I." Eventually they will pay the price.

8. God's truths work whether we are atheist or devoted Christian. He loves each of us whether we know Him or not.

False Gods: Sins of the Heart

Problem: The "spiritual vacuum" causes us to seek God, yet, misinformed and unaware, many of us get trapped into worshipping false idols instead.

Causes: Insecurities, deceit, fear, seeds of pain in the heart, bad habits, wrong role models and culture, and sins of our parents.

Outward Confirmations: Denial, defensiveness, blaming others, physical appearance, hiding the truth, wrong habits.

Healing Occurs Through: Admitting a problem, forgiveness, prayer (asking for help), immersion in the Word of God, counseling, fellowship, support groups, divine forgiveness, and love, love and love...through a personal relationship with Christ and the spirit of God flowing through you.

Failure Leads To Success

Movement To And From His Truths

Focus:

Others
⇧
Love
⇧
Faith
⇧
Him

Seeking The Higher Purpose

Consequences:

Blessings
⇧
Purpose
⇧
Joy
⇧
Peace

Peace, joy, magnify
Receives peace, new direction
Receives brokenness
Grows closer to Him
Patient, repenting
Counsels with peers, seeks advice
Allows himself to be vulnerable
Seeks forgiveness, prayers of others
Study the word, fellowship

Spiritual Truth:
Have No False Idols

Self focus for pleasure
Fear of Failure
Tension, frustration, hurt
Depends on vices
Driven to work hard, as answer
Defensive, covers up to look good
Trapped in false god, habits, closed heart
Blame others

Focus:

Self
⇩
Negatives
⇩
Works
⇩
Fear

Falling To Deeper Depths

Consequences:

Unrestful
⇩
Stress
⇩
Pain
⇩
Sickness

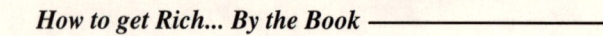

WORDS ARE THE SEEDS OF LIFE

Spiritual Truth: *Don't use God's name in vain*

Character Quality: *But instead praise with your tongue*

Words to the Heart

Sister Helen Mrosla isn't famous or world renowned but her story is something that would touch anyone's heart. In her first year of teaching in Morris, Minnesota, her third grade class had a number of rowdy kids who seemed to continually pick on each other and make fun of one another. She became so frustrated that she decided to take positive action.

She took single sheets of notebook paper and wrote the name of each student at the top. As she passed around each paper she asked every student to write one positive thing about every other student on their paper as it went around the room. It took practically the whole afternoon but it seemed to change the tone of the class and set a proper atmosphere for the rest of the school year.

But that is only half the story. Ten years later one of the students from that class died in the Vietnam War. At his funeral, the young man's father stood up and showed everyone a worn and tattered piece of notebook paper. It had obviously been folded and refolded and had some old scotch tape holding it together where it had been torn. It was the list that the boy had been given by his classmates in the third grade. He had kept it all those years.

"His Commanding Officer found it on my son's body after he died," the father said. *"He kept it in his shirt pocket so that he could pull it out and read it whenever he was feeling blue."* Sister Helen, who repeated the story years later in <u>Reader's Digest</u>, noted that there were four other classmates from that particular class at the funeral. Three of them had kept their list all those years. Encouraging words can make a dramatic impact on the life of another person.

CHARACTER QUALITY

-*Praise with your tongue* -

Words are thoughts and containers filled with emotions, meanings, mental pictures, information and direction that are planted and grow in our hearts (spirit) and dictate our emotions. Scripture refers to the tongue and its words as a rudder on a ship; with the slightest turn it changes directions and moves the body, soul and spirit.

"Don't use God's name in vain" has a deeper meaning, beyond merely refraining from profanity. Dr. Robert Schuller says "The gift of words are to be used to communicate respect to the rest of the members of the human family to the end and for the purpose of creating mutual affirming and enriching relationships.

When language is used to insult, ridicule, embarrass, demean, belittle or dishonor another member of the family, we put stress on ourselves and relationships. In the end God's name is the head of the family and the name of every other member of the human family are disgraced. Precious relationships are not enriched, rather they are deprived of dignity and left impoverished."

You can tell the depth of a man's or woman's character by the choice of their words...not by their length or vocabulary...but their respect, attitude and motives.

Very few of us stop to realize that words are spiritual, as well as mental and physical in nature and control our interactions and relationships with Him and our fellowman.

Words Are The Seeds Of Life

Words Hold Power

If you were asked the provocative question, "What is the most powerful instrument or influence in the world," what would you say? God used His tongue to create the whole earth and used the words,"*Let there by light,*" to speak light and life into existence. As Dr. Robert Schuller says, "*Because God, the Creator, designed the human being in His image, bearing His honored name, we are designed to become co-creators with Him. Words hold the power to creativity. Creative words generate energy; negative words drain out energy. A single word can turn you on, or it can turn you off. Negative words can diffuse your enthusiasm for a project. A positive word releases positive energy and becomes a creative force.*"

"Many men forget God all day and ask Him to remember them at night."

WORDS

A careless word — may kindle strife,
A cruel word — may wreck a life,
A bitter word — may hate instill,
A brutal word — may smite and kill.
A gracious word — may smooth the way,
A joyous word — may light the day.
A timely word — may lessen stress,
A loving word — may heal and bless.

(*The War Cry*)

Words of Creativity

Have you ever been in a task force meeting in a corporation when somebody offered a particularly creative idea? There seems to be an excitement, enthusiasm and an energy flow because of the uniqueness of the idea. Then somebody says, *"Look, guys, what you are proposing doesn't make any sense at all and won't work because we tried that three years ago."* Those words can deplete enthusiasm, morale and even create bitterness and jealousy, even though they may not have intended to do so. But, nevertheless, the energy is totally drained by the negative statement of one person. This helps each of us understand why in every brainstorming meeting the facilitator says, *"There are no bad ideas, so save your criticism until I call for them."*

Words Affect Our Health

Doug Leatherdale, President and CEO of St. Paul Companies, reported that *"The American Medical Association estimates that 80% or more of medical problems are stress related. The estimated cost is $50 billion annually."* Charles Mayo, who cofounded the Mayo Clinic, says, *"Worry affects circulation, heart, glands and the whole nervous system. I have never known a man who died from overwork, but a lot who died from doubt."*

Scripture says that words are seeds that are planted in our heart. Words express emotions and take root in our spirit or heart. It is the emotions of words that create joy, peace, doubt or worry in our life. Negative words create stress, and stress leads to sickness or ill health.

Dr. Ken Cooper, who coined the phrase, *Aerobics*, and author of many best sellers, says that there are two basic kinds of belief from the scientific point of view. The first is extrinsic belief, almost a rote or mechanical affirmation of convictions of spiritual faith. He says, *"The distinguishing feature of this sort of belief is that it remains in the head and never makes it to the heart. Various studies prove that this type of belief does not improve a person's spiritual status, emotional well-being, or physical health.*

Intrinsic belief is characterized by a spiritual commitment to the meaning of life, heartfelt prayer and a quest to be changed. This kind of inner conviction — which may be accompanied by, but never limited to, outward, external observance is the key to real spiritual power." Real spiritual power is rooted in and created by the Word of God.

Decision Making

By God's design, seeds planted in fertile soil produce fruit...sometimes sweet (like flowers and strawberries), sometimes bitter or even poisonous (like weeds and poison berries). The Bible says words are the seeds of our heart or spirit. Positive words are continuously filled with faith, meanings, solutions and willingness to take risks. Positive words are sweet and produce fruits of love, joy, contentment and peace. Bitter words produce hurt, depression, frustration or even hate. The interpretation of words are the result of life's learning experiences, attitude, faith and even inheritance.

Brian Tracey, internationally known author, trainer and consultant from San Diego, says, *"100% of our decisions are based on our emotions."* Our emotions are controlled by our heart and the positive or negative meaning inside us. As we make a decision it runs by our brain and heart simultaneously. The brain, which is the soul, may say "good idea" and the heart (spirit) says "watch out for hurt." Hurt or unforgiven are slow to go away without God's influence.

We can't make a decision without the words we receive being interrupted, judged and give a heart-felt response. It is impossible to be fully objective unless we can remove our emotions, which is impossible to do.

> *"Any fool can count the seeds in an apple. Only God can count the apples in one seed."*
> **Robert Schuller**

Love or Perish

It is continually recognized by physicians and scholars that our heart or spirit is tied directly to the root of our sickness, diseases or peace. In the book, <u>None of These Diseases</u>, by S. I. McMillen, M.D. and Dr. E. Stern, M.D., the chapter on "Love or Perish" focuses on what he terms the psychosomatic illnesses. There are a number of carnal attitudes and emotions which come from the seeds of negative words that we place in our heart and get translated into stress or illness.

Dr. McMillen uses a list of corresponding diseases which cause emotions that he has extracted from a noted psychiatric textbook. Psychiatrist, Smiley Blanton, says, *"Without love, thoughtfulness and keen consideration of others — we become much more likely to perish from a variety of diseases of the body and mind."* He continued by quoting international psychiatrist, Alfred Adler, *"The most important task imposed by religion has always been **love thy neighbor**...it is the individual who is not interested in his fellowman who has the greatest difficulties in life and provides the greatest injury to others. It is from such individuals that all human failings spring."* Dr. Adler based his conclusions on a careful analysis of thousands of patients. He held that the lack of love was responsible for "all human failures."

"When I quote the Bible," reports Dr. Adler, *"to patients who are suffering physically and mentally from the lack of love, some of them retort that it is very difficult to change one's feeling — to change hate to love."* That is true. Psychologists support this view, for we, as humans, cannot gain complete control of our feelings. Yet, psychologists also state that our will can control our actions. *"What we will to do is usually what we will do. Our will can give us freedom from bondage to our fickle emotions."*

Notice that there is one word which overcomes all the negative attitudes that produce disease. The word is "***Love***" with all its meanings. As you study this, you will soon realize "Love" is the most important word, seed, emotion and container. God created us in Love, protects and forgives us out of Love and sent His only son to die for us out of Love.

When Jesus was asked what was the greatest commandment of all, He said, *"**Love** your Lord God with all your heart, soul and might, and **Love** your neighbor as yourself."* God loved us enough to create us and then send His only son. He invented **Love**. He is the only true source of **Love**. We must seek Him to receive His full measure in our lives and then we will start to radiate it to others.

The following chart compares the definition of Love from the Bible with corresponding disease-causing emotions directly from Dr. Kolb's textbook.

*LOVE	ATTITUDES THAT PRODUCE DISEASE
Is patient.	Frustration Discontent
Is kind.	Aggressiveness
Does not envy.	Envy Jealousy
Does not boast	Seeking attention
Is not proud	Over-valued body concept
Is not rude	Taking attitude
Is not self-seeking	Selfishness Greed
Is not easily angered	Anger Rage Irritableness
Keeps no record of wrong	Resentment Hatred
Does not delight in evil	Death wishes for others Sexual fantasies
Rejoices with the truth	Dejection Desperation
Always protects	Competitiveness
Always trusts	Anxiety Doubt Striving for security Paranoia
Always hopes	Fear Despair Discouragement
Always perseveres	Irresponsibility Apathy

* I Corinthians 13:4

How to get Rich... By the Book

The Garden of Our Heart and Spirit

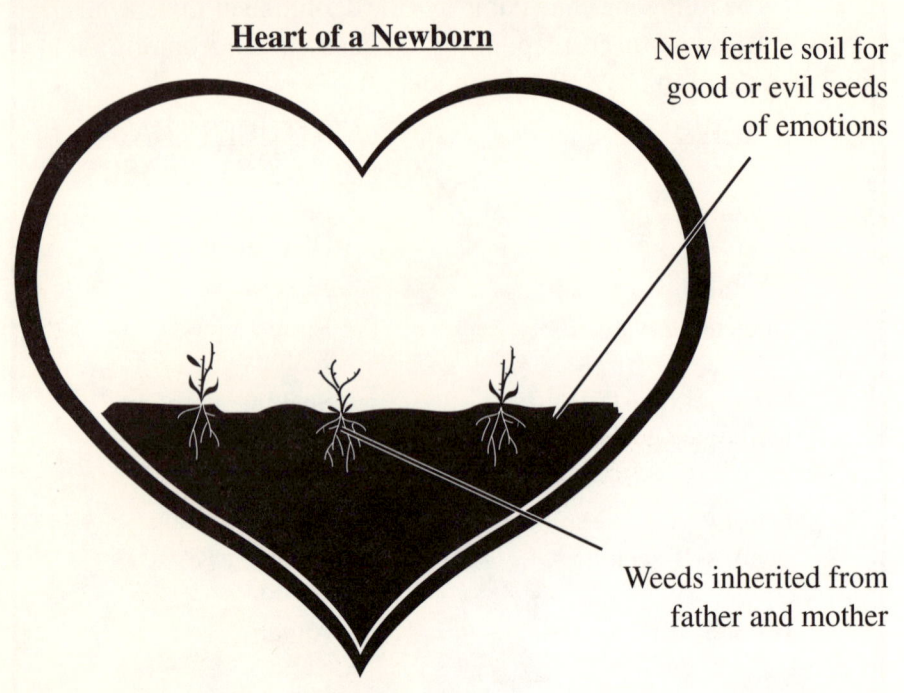

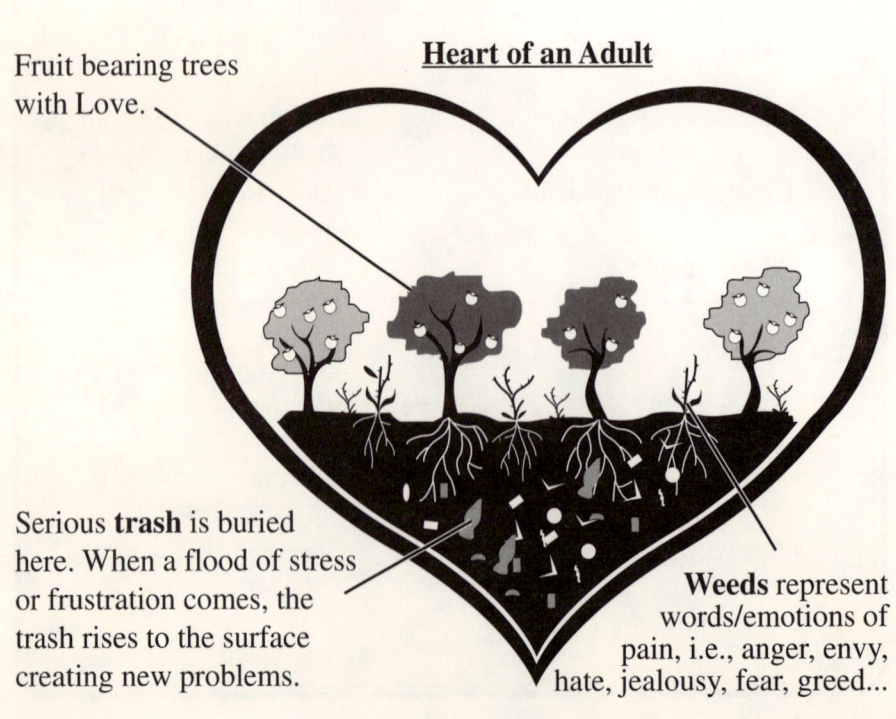

Heart of a Newborn

New fertile soil for good or evil seeds of emotions

Weeds inherited from father and mother

Heart of an Adult

Fruit bearing trees with Love.

Serious **trash** is buried here. When a flood of stress or frustration comes, the trash rises to the surface creating new problems.

Weeds represent words/emotions of pain, i.e., anger, envy, hate, jealousy, fear, greed...

Words of Love bear fruit -- take root, i.e. kindness, patience, giving, humble, faith, hope...

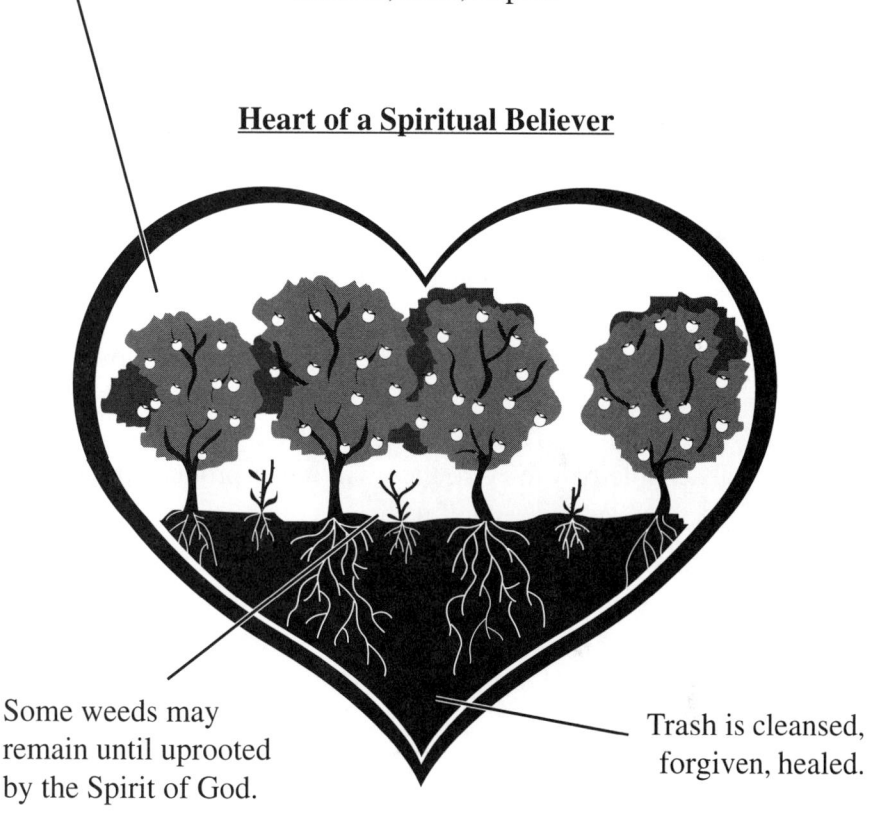

Heart of a Spiritual Believer

Some weeds may remain until uprooted by the Spirit of God.

Trash is cleansed, forgiven, healed.

The Word of God Heals and Nourishes

Fruit bearing seeds nurtured and growing can choke off weeds... the Bible is the source of love, truth and spiritual growth.

The amount of hurt or love in our heart controls our emotions, attitudes and decision making. Only the loving word of God can heal us of the hurt planted there.

Love produces sweet fruit of kindness, patience, forgiveness, joy, peace... to give unselfishly and receive back with humility.

THE MORAL OF THE STORIES:

1. The spirit and depth of His truth is that God used the seed of His words to create earth and life. Used against His truths, they harm. Used in harmony with His truths, they are words, thoughts and emotions that command and lead our lives in goodness.

2. Proverbs says, *"As a man thinketh <u>in his heart</u>, so is he."* We think first with our heart and emotions, then with our brain.

3. The body is fed with food. The mind is fed with knowledge, communication and mental stimulation. The heart is fed with words and the emotions they represent.

4. There is only one source of words that heal, build, love, restore, and forgive. Those words are written by the author of our creation in scripture. Without being humble, open and teachable before Him, they will never produce the full love he intended for each of us.

5. Words put our emotions on an upward or downward cycle in life. They command spiritual life and death. They allow the word of God to penetrate the heart through study and fellowship and stabilize our emotions through His love.

6. Scripture words are more blessed than money. They buy peace, joy, fulfillment, and healing of the heart — eternal things that last forever. Words of hate do the opposite and cause harm, pain, and kill the human spirit. Unfortunately the person who holds hate, bitterness, jealousy and envy in their hearts toward another person robs their heart of joy. It hurts them far more inside that the person that they hate. The demise of our human values is a result of our ignorance toward our Creator's design and lessened opportunities to reach our hearts.

7. Words command body, soul and spiritual movements. Our choice of words is critical. This is where the Power of Positive Mental Thinking is derived.

8. While food, sleep and exercise are critical to the body's healing, most sickness can be traced to stress (created by the

Words Are The Seeds Of Life

negative consequences of words/thoughts and actions). They place undue stress on an organ, or system of the body. It is like a balloon that has to burst from the stress of too much air. The peace of mind that only God can give overcomes stress.

9. Bullets, AIDS, and drugs can kill your body but not your spirit. However, words can kill the spirit or they can bring life.
10. If we seek peace of mind, without knowing Him, we find temporary comfort in the words of a novel, movie or friend, attempting to fill the void. The deeper our emotional hurt and experiences they represent, the stronger some people go to seek out sex, violence, or revenge.

What Is An Attitude

It is the "advance man" of our true selves.
Its roots are inward but its fruit is outward.
It is our best friend or our worst enemy.
It is more honest and more consistent than our words.
It is an outward look based on past experiences.
It is a thing which draws people to us or repels them.
It is never content until it is expressed.
It is the librarian of our past.
It is the speaker of our present.
It is the prophet of our future.

How to get Rich... By the Book

Movement To And From His Truths

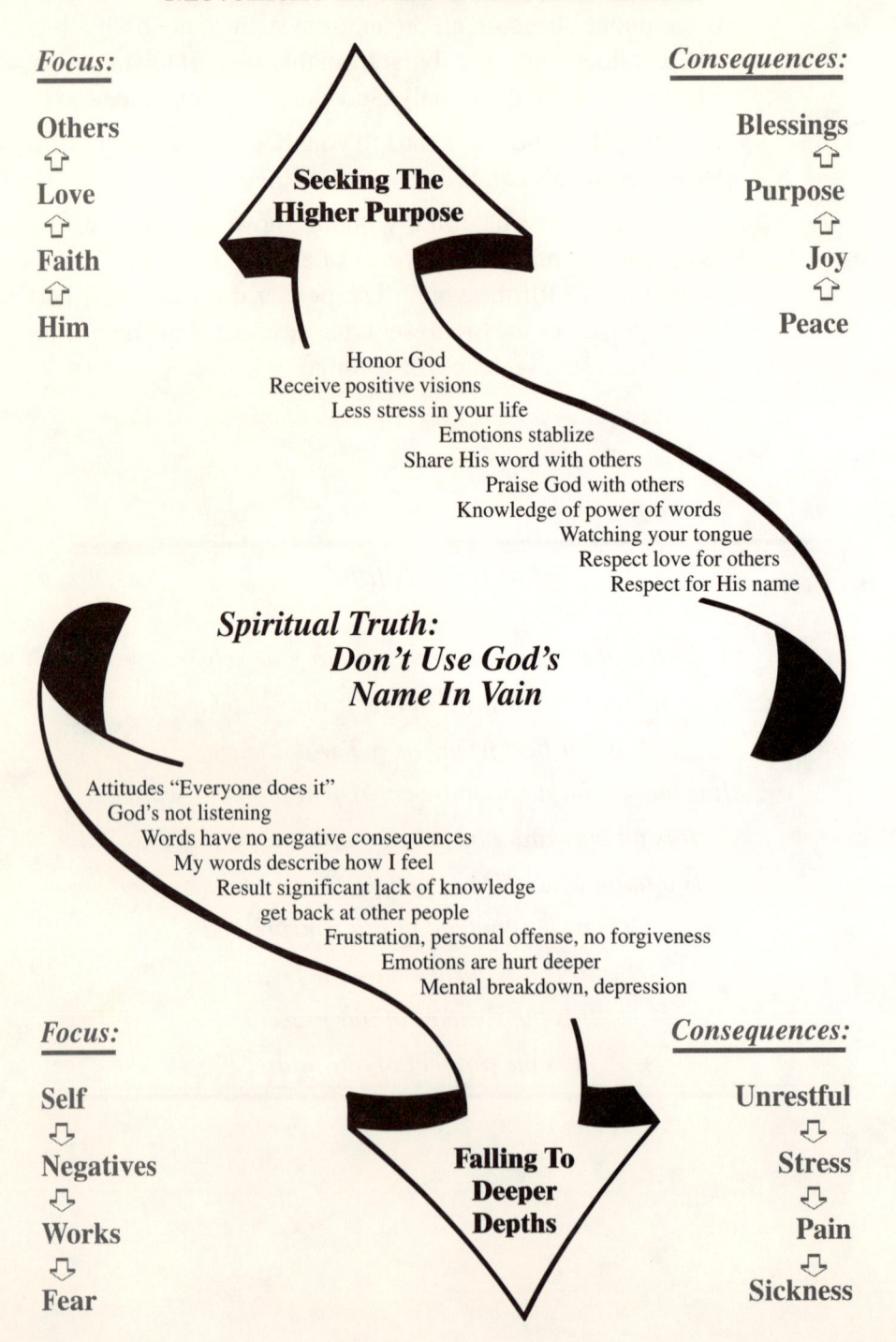

Focus:

Others
⇧
Love
⇧
Faith
⇧
Him

Seeking The Higher Purpose

Consequences:

Blessings
⇧
Purpose
⇧
Joy
⇧
Peace

Honor God
Receive positive visions
Less stress in your life
Emotions stablize
Share His word with others
Praise God with others
Knowledge of power of words
Watching your tongue
Respect love for others
Respect for His name

Spiritual Truth:
Don't Use God's
Name In Vain

Attitudes "Everyone does it"
God's not listening
Words have no negative consequences
My words describe how I feel
Result significant lack of knowledge
get back at other people
Frustration, personal offense, no forgiveness
Emotions are hurt deeper
Mental breakdown, depression

Focus:

Self
⇩
Negatives
⇩
Works
⇩
Fear

Falling To Deeper Depths

Consequences:

Unrestful
⇩
Stress
⇩
Pain
⇩
Sickness

90

THE PROBLEM WITH RELIGION

Spiritual Truth: *Keep the Sabbath Holy*

Character Quality: *By resting and listening in Me*

Lead Us Father

Not everyone recognizes Grant Teaff, Executive Director of the American Football Coaches Association and former head coach of the Baylor University Football Team. In 1963 he was head coach of the McMurry College Indians, and they had just lost a game in Monroe, Louisiana. They had chartered a plane and were heading back with heads hung low in disappointment. Things seemed unusual when the pilot did not return on time. Just after they took off, the pilot decided he was going to swing back and land. As he returned for the landing the plane bounced back into the air again. One propeller and the landing gear were broken. The pilot came back to Grant and told him that they were going to go on to Shreveport (SAC Base) and attempt to make a crash landing.

There was utter silence on the plane. The lights were lost. Finally one of the boys turned to Grant and said, *"Coach, will you lead us in prayer?"* So he said in prayer as everyone held tight, *"God, You have a plan, purpose and will for our lives and if You will spare our lives we will do everything in our power to fulfill Your plan."* As he said that prayer, his own life flashed before him, his wife, his family and his relationship to God.

The plane crashed and caught fire but miraculously everyone escaped without harm. The anxious news media wanted the story but Grant simply told them that "God has got a plan for our lives." The next day as the team assembled, one of the boys suggested that they form a club and vow to stay in contact so they could see what God does with each of their individual lives.

He comically wanted to call the club the "Brotherhood of Indian Belly Landing Experts." They ordered cards with the club name but the printer had to abbreviate the name. When they received the cards, they were pleasantly surprised that they were known as the BIBLE Club.

At the 20 year reunion, not one of the men had been divorced, and they are all serving God in some capacity.

"When you're green you're growing, when you're ripe you're rotten."

CHARACTER QUALITY

- Rest and listen in Me -

To look like Mr. Universe or Miss America, in addition to good genes, you need the right balance of diet and exercise. We all recognize that it takes a certain discipline to gain the right figure or improve the look of the body. Yet if we would like to be as smart as Albert Einstein and weren't born with the same mental genius then our next best alternative is to start reading, learning, listening and researching. We would be filling our brain with every fact, figure and bit of information that would help us accomplish our mental goals.

It is the same for a spiritual journey with God. It requires exercising our spirit through a relationship with Him pursuing personal growth, Sunday worship, reading our Bible, fellowshipping with others and seeking His direction.

This is the very principle that God is laying out for each of us with this truth. It is not about religion; it is about a personal relationship with Him. It is not about doing the right works but about grace and faith.

Growth is one of the keys to life. It starts with the seed word of God that brings peace to your heart.

─────────────────────────────────── *The Problem With Religion*

> *"If you put money in savings it grows, if you put money in the offering plate you grow."*

Russian Faith

Dr. Robert Schuller shares the story of Walter Anderson, the editor of Parade Magazine. *"Walter came from the poor side of New York City and as a child was abused by an angry father. Considering Walter's negative home and childhood, he had no interest in a heavenly father, churches, a religion, especially since he had a fill of his earthly father. On his own he had managed fine by himself; he had no need for a belief system."*

That all changed when he met God in, of all places, a Russian cathedral before the fall of the Iron Curtain, as an American tourist. This is how he related the incident:

"About 25 miles south of Moscow is a little cathedral called the Church of the Trinity. It is a Russian Orthodox church. I visited this little cathedral and was struck by the rope that ran down the center of the church. On one side were people who viewed the cathedral as a museum. On the other side were people who were believers. I was with a monk named Longin.

I heard this beautiful hymn — it was magnificent. I couldn't recognize it, but it touched me. Being a typical American, I looked to see where the choir was. I couldn't figure it out. I couldn't believe this beautiful hymn. Finally I asked Longin, "Where is the choir?"

Longin replied, "As the believers come in they pick up the sound of the hymn, and as they leave, they stop so there is always, here in Russia, a continuing hymn."

I thought about these people who profess their belief and stand for what they believe — in a society which ridiculed the notion of God, which discouraged religion in nearly every form.

Still they stand; they continue to believe, and I asked Longin, 'How did you come to be a priest, a monk? How did you even learn to do this?'

'When I was a child,' he said, 'we were taught the stories of the Bible as legends.

All of the students read them as legends and myths. Then there came a moment when I read the stories differently; I believed them; I heard them differently from the other children.'

When Longin said that it came to me that I now heard the stories differently, and I too believed."

"God speaks to those who take time to listen."

Vaccinated Christians

In a country like ours founded by men with a deep Christian belief, many Americans have been brought up in or attended church. Since spirituality is not physical and visible it is not real to many who are too intelligent to believe in God. Besides, society doesn't seem to emphasize it at work or at play. People know the story of Christ and see Him as a nice historical figure. Surveys confirm that 90% of Americans believe in a God and many say *"I'm a good person, isn't that enough?"* They might say, *"I live by the Ten Commandments - I've never killed anyone, committed adultery and don't steal."* Others see Christians as hypocritical, acting one way in church but another way during the week. Others are turned off by the words, "King" and "Lord," after all those are medieval terms of repressors who controlled the peasants, when in truth it means leader. Some say Christianity is boring, anti-fun and can't compete with the Sunday morning entertainment found on television, movies, football or even golf.

Let it be known by all, that all types of believers and nonbelievers fall short of His plan and purposes. The word "sin" comes from the archers of medieval times when an archer "missed the mark." Even the best Christian has "missed the mark" and unfortunately, given a world full of evil, we are all hypocrites, and will sin again. Yet, we can be forgiven through Christ. Religion is not the answer, it is man made with our faults. The answer is a personal relationship with God through Jesus Christ.

Amazing Grace

Ken Blanchard, co-author of <u>The One-Minute Manager</u> shares how he and his wife made a significant mistake in their early career by being

The Problem With Religion

a church drop-out. Ken was teaching at Ohio University and the pastor of their church, whom they really appreciated, was fired. He had become involved in student protests over the Vietnam war. He shares that, *"Anger and disillusionment came crashing in on us. We thought 'If that's what church is all about, forget it.' We dropped out. Like so many people, we went to church only at Christmas and Easter for fifteen years."*

Years later, Ken sought a desire to know more about God sensing a need for a greater purpose and peace. The tremendous success of his books and company were not providing a sense of fulfillment. He talked with his good friend Bob Buford, a successful CEO and himself an author. Ken could not see himself as a sinner. Bob explained it this way, *"Ken, do you see yourself as good as God?"* Ken said, *"No, God is perfect."* Bob continued *"Okay. On a scale of 1 to 100, let's give God 100. We'll give Mother Teresa 90 and a murderer 5. Ken, you are a decent sort and trying to help others. I'll give you 75. Now the special thing about Christianity is that God sent Jesus to make up the difference between you and 100. That's what grace is all about. It is not about deeds. If you accept Jesus as your Savior, no matter what your past has been, He rids you of your sins and brings you closer to 100."*

Ken realized that he wrongfully viewed God in a religious context, thinking about doing good by achievement would bring him fulfillment and even get him into Heaven. Now, he often asks people in his management seminars these questions:

> How many of you have children?
>
> How many love those children?
>
> How many love your children dependent upon their achievement?

They all admit that they would love their children whether they are high achievers or not. That's the way God is as well. He offers unconditional love.

Ken offers this view *"If we can begin to accept unconditional love from our Father, we set the stage for acknowledging grace. Your focus no longer has to be out there with results, accumulation, power, acceptance, control, or earthly things. Now you can focus on your own sense of personal excellence and the journey – how to live your life. You can begin to live according to God's law."*

Religion is the Law Created by Man

Nowhere in the Bible does it say that God asks us to create churches with different denominations and doctrines. Pete Maravich said, *"Religion sends more people to hell — denominations, religions and false religions. Christianity is the truth. Christianity is not a 100 yard dash, it is a marathon and just keeps going on and on."* Through man's different levels of understandings, style, personality, personal growth, training or visions, different denominations have been created. Each Christian is on a personal journey, a walk with God and He leads us through our different stages of growth, dependent on our openness and commitment. This is where Christians appear hypocritical to the uninformed or non-believer. The Bible is the common foundation and source for our Christian faith.

Dr. Ken Cooper talked about "extrinsic belief" and we see that type of belief in Northern Ireland where the Protestants battle Catholics, also in Bosnia and former Yugoslavian Republics, and in the Middle East, only to name a few. Those countries are being torn apart by religious strife. America has been blessed by God and our founders in that we have avoided religious wars because most of us have been taught The Ten Commandments and to respect and honor freedom of religion and denominations. The American spiritual battle is for the heart, the difference between truth and deceit, good and bad, jealousy, greed, and revenge, to name a few. The Great Crusades of Europe choked off the real spiritual opportunities to penetrate the hearts and develop intrinsic believers.

Yet the most respected woman in the world, Mother Teresa, from European Yugoslavia, honors and serves God and is a shining example of giving her best to honor Him. Others need to follow her example.

"In Calcutta, people are starving physically. In America, people are starving emotionally. What people are hungering for is Love, that only God can provide."

Mother Teresa

Lack of Spiritual Growth Can Produce:

—Emptiness
—Frustrations and tension
—Deep hunger for something unknown
—Great desire to be loved
—Economic stress
—Money with no joy or peace
—Failure, lack of success
—Physical pain, sickness
—Accidents
—Loss of job, loved one

Four Types of Believers

Generally, there are four different stages, levels of belief, or combination that helps to categorize and explain where people are in relationship to the Christian faith:

1. Non-believer — raised in the home where there is no basis for moral values, attitudes focus on entitlement, "take what you can get," family love is absent, and very little respect for authority is practiced. God is not important if He even exists.

2. Self-believer — To be successful you have got to "do it your way," work hard within the system but use it for your own personal gain. If you can't see God, He must not be real, or care. The self-made goal is to seek your own personal satisfaction and "look out for number one."

3. Moral believer — Concerned about others, as well as self, and believes in God, particularly as a last resort. Attends church and believes in moral values. The goal is to be a good person, successful, and a contributor to society. If asked by the boss, he will go along with breaking some ethics or policies. Sees God by the size and shape of his level of faith.

4. Spiritual believer — Seeks God's love, direction and will through a personal commitment. Sees his life as a spiritual journey, driven by God's values. Openly seeks and learns through the Bible, sharing with other Christians, through

prayer, and fellowship. As he sees God working in his life, he gives Him credit. He understands the true meaning of love because the flow of God's love works through his life. He is God-centered and people-centered.

All four of these types of people have a little overlap as we are always learning, growing, changing, and hopefully moving closer toward the spiritual Christian that God is calling all of us to become. The Spiritual Christian, as he grows and sincerely comprehends God's purpose in his life, has more vision, joy and sense of fulfillment, and is not as concerned about material things.

"Don't be just a teacher, be a student teacher."

Why Go to Church?

Bill McCombes, President of Infoquest, says "It's just a matter of perspective and how much you want to experience. For example, if someone asks you what happened with your favorite team, you have 5 ways to know:
  a. Hear the score
  b. Read about it in the paper
  c. Watch it on TV
  d. Sit in the stadium; or
  e. Playing, taking action in the event, being part of the team.

Obviously, church is best when we are a participant and we grow by the experience.

"Some people complain because God put thorns on the roses, while others praise Him for putting roses among thorns."

Beyond Church

Tom Landry, the Hall of Fame football coach of the Dallas Cowboys, and Bernhard Langer, two time winner of the Masters Golf Tournament, have something in common. One was raised a Protestant and the other a Catholic, and both attended church every Sunday. Their common thread is that a friend invited them to a Bible Study. They each believed attending church made them a Christian. After all, they believed in God.

They both confessed that attending that Bible Study opened their eyes, ears and hearts to a whole new journey and commitment to the Lord. Meeting Him brought joy, peace and understanding they had never known before, especially in their stressful athletic careers with the pressure they had both faced. They understood the old adage that "parking yourself in a garage does not make you a car," any more than attending church makes you a Christian. It takes faith and commitment to expand our journey in life.

Sharing Faith

"The greatest decision I ever made as a coach," says Florida State Coach Bobby Bowden, *"was instituting a daily devotional with our coaches and staff. We meet for staff meetings every morning and take five minutes before we get started and a different member shares a Biblical truth or motivating statement that will help each one of us grow personally."*

Every Friday night before a game there is a team dinner and Bobby shares Scripture or a personal message about his walk with the Lord. He reminds the players that life after football is a real challenge and that each of us needs a "rock" to be anchored to. While Bowden has had a number of players drafted in the NFL, he reminds them that the average stay is only four years.

Tom Osborne and his staff at Nebraska and hundreds of other coaches around the country are involved in FCA (Fellowship of Christian Athletes, headquartered in Kansas City) and share their stories and help young men and women from high school to professionals become prepared for a life that is eternal.

Walk Their Talk

Truett Cathy, the founder of Chick-Fil-A, has personally been involved in leading a Sunday School class in his church for over 40 years. Bo Pilgrim, Founder of the Pilgrim Pride Company (a $1 billion chicken processing business) has taught Sunday School for 24 years and has built a prayer tower open to the public in his home town of Pittsburg, Texas. He also provides 45 different chaplains through the Marketplace Ministries organization of Dallas, Texas, to his 6,000 employees in four different plants. Gil Stricklin, former staff member of the Billy Graham organization, is founder of this group that trains and supplies over 275 part-time pastors to companies in the Southeast and Northeast.(Also note chapter 9). Truett Cathy has built a large camp for boys and girls and personally sponsors 45 foster children in five different homes. He also provides up to $10,000 in college scholarships for kids that work in his business.

> *"God blesses people and businesses who honor Him."*

Returning Your Call

Did you ever have a friend who only calls when he needs something, yet never really offers to return the favor, or seem appreciative? Even if you have a heart to want to help, it can be annoying sometimes. Often you will stop returning their calls.

Well, our Creator has the same nature. We were created in His image. That is why He wants a personal relationship. Yes, He will respond to an emergency or "House Call" in answering our prayers, but at the same time, that may be why He doesn't return our calls or answer our prayers. He is tired of being our "genie" — the magic lamp we use when we want something big.

We appreciate those most whom we can give to and give back. He is no different and that is one of the reasons He seeks a personal relationship to go beyond the need to be the god of emergencies and become the God of a daily walk together. He desires to give and take in love and kindness, in little requests as well as large ones.

Is it any wonder why so many "good" people may not make it to Heaven?

Five Ways He Talks To Us

1. The Holy Spirit touches our heart...i.e., a soft inner voice or a real peace and calm from reading His Word. We gain wisdom, understanding, direction or insight as a result.
2. Through a friend, boss, spouse, employee or associate who gives us advice (often a confirmation or realization of His truth or direction for you).
3. Warning signs - early indicators, a lack of peace of mind about trouble ahead.
4. Wake-up calls...profound problems or frustrations which occur because we are "missing the mark" or misguided...He is waiting for us to turn back to His truths.
5. Failures or tragedies that ultimately seem to mature us and bring us back to Him in a humble way.

God protects moral people for a "grace period" of time but will allow us to suffer the consequences of our negative actions. It is always a learning experience for us. Many of the experiences are humbling. If we don't humble ourselves before God and seek Him, He will encourage our humility.

THE MORAL OF THE STORIES:

1. The Lord is <u>not</u> calling us to a religion or denomination but to a personal relationship with Him.
2. Keeping the Sabbath holy is about drawing us closer to Him with a restful and open heart. Set aside restful time to praise, pray, reflect and grow closer to Him.
3. Each of the first four commandments of The Ten Commandments is about having a personal relationship and walk with Christ. Churches or organizations which fail to

teach these principles are missing the fulfillment of God's spiritual truths.

4. The Bible speaks to the spirit of man, we must be "born of the spirit" for the Word to become personally meaningful and reveal His truth.

5. All of us "miss the mark" (sin) and fall short of His righteousness in our lives, but through the urging of the Holy Spirit we will continue to grow more like Him.

6. The Bible says *"My people perish from a lack of knowledge,"* so we must take the time to read His word, to find truth for the direction and purpose of our lives.

7. Moses brought the Truths of God, The Ten Commandments, down from the mountain top to the Jewish people who sought the "truths for success" in their new found freedom. Jesus brought the "Spirit of the Truth" with a further explanation and understanding of the how, why and where of God's commands. His death was a sacrifice for our sins and our inability to measure up to His righteousness. But the journey continues as we grow closer to Him.

The Problem With Religion

Movement To And From His Truths

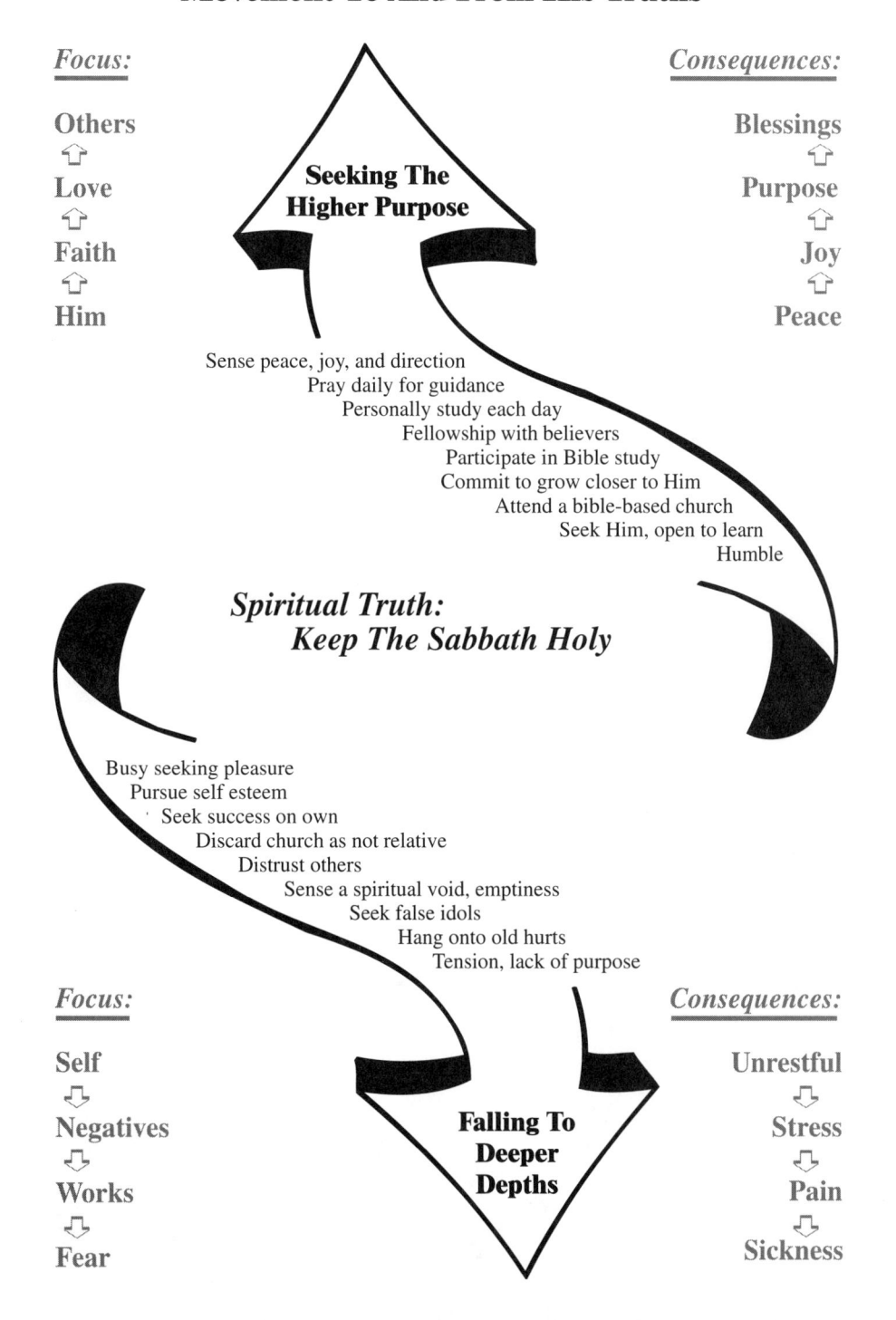

Focus:

Others
⇧
Love
⇧
Faith
⇧
Him

Seeking The Higher Purpose

Consequences:

Blessings
⇧
Purpose
⇧
Joy
⇧
Peace

Sense peace, joy, and direction
Pray daily for guidance
Personally study each day
Fellowship with believers
Participate in Bible study
Commit to grow closer to Him
Attend a bible-based church
Seek Him, open to learn
Humble

Spiritual Truth: Keep The Sabbath Holy

Busy seeking pleasure
Pursue self esteem
Seek success on own
Discard church as not relative
Distrust others
Sense a spiritual void, emptiness
Seek false idols
Hang onto old hurts
Tension, lack of purpose

Focus:

Self
⇩
Negatives
⇩
Works
⇩
Fear

Falling To Deeper Depths

Consequences:

Unrestful
⇩
Stress
⇩
Pain
⇩
Sickness

Moral Truths

The last six truths of the Ten Commandments are guidelines for loving our fellowman. The Lord embodied them when He said to "Love your neighbor as yourself." Also known as the golden rule is "Do unto others as you would have them do unto you."

These truths have become the most widely accepted foundations for business ethics in America with growing acceptance throughout the world.

As businesses and individuals continue to learn ways to love (care, empathy, listening and servicing their needs), their neighbor (employees, customers, suppliers, vendors, community and stockholders)...plus using their God given talents by His will, they shall become more richly blessed.

Being "customer focused" was His design long before the CEOs, business authors, consultants and professors discovered it as the central way to succeed in business.

9

WE ARE FAMILY BY DESIGN

Moral Truth: *Honor father and mother*

Character Quality: *By respecting authority as family*

Family Values

James Cash Penney, a mentor to many executives in and out of his own company, enjoyed sharing the story of how as a young man he lived on a farm in Missouri. His father struggled in farming and also served as the unpaid pastor of the local church. One day his father asked the elders of the church if they would consider paying him for his time and services. The elders called an inquisition with an open discussion that Jim and his mother could witness as his father explained his need. Many elders were upset because a pastor had never been paid in their church before. As they voted against his father's request, they asked him to resign.

Afterward his father never wavered or held a grudge. That example taught Jim a great lesson that influenced his entire life. He would take "The Golden Rule," as his father taught him, to its full intent. Put the customers' needs first and maintain a forgiving attitude should they not be satisfied.

After his great success, Jim Penney built a retirement home for retired pastors in North Florida in memory of his father and mother. It is still in operation today. He never forgot the example and truths his mother and father taught him.

Jim Penney told executives that he believed that the best course for business is the "Sermon on the Mount" found in the Book of Matthew.

How to get Rich... By the Book

"If we just follow the principles of Christ we will win the loyalty of our customer, go the second mile, give and it will be given back to us, and we will serve well. In the long run we will win many friends."

CHARACTER QUALITY

- Respect authority as family-

The Lord chose a father and mother to represent a family unit for the conception and nurturing of each of us. The root of our values comes from our family. The family gives us our name and heritage. It represents those in authority above us who are to be respected. The family is our emotional stronghold where we must learn to forgive, become good stewards and eventually better and more loving parents ourselves.

Businesses are an extended family for employees, especially for those who come from broken homes and who never learned the basic values He intended. Employees who have had problems with their parents and failed to learn respect for authority bring the same attitude into the work environment. Every business teaches truth or values. The question is whether they also "walk their talk." What eternal truths does your business teach? Since every life is eternal, how we respect and influence our families can live forever.

The Business Family

Norm Miller is CEO of Interstate Batteries, a $500 million company based in Dallas, Texas. He selected Jim Coté to be his Chaplain and created a department to offer spiritual counseling to, not only the employees, but distributors and their families as part of the Interstate greater organization.

Jim believes that the CEOs of today are the bishops of tomorrow." His company department distributes 200,000 newsletters a year, provides

We Are Family By Design

a complete library of books and reference materials for family and personal issues, leads requested Bible Study and does individual counseling in person or by phone. More recently they developed a whole video counseling series entitled "Marriage and the Road" for couples who have to be gone from the home for extended periods of time.

More and more companies are moving to the chaplain concept as they help their employees deal with personal or family issues because it impacts work and their character. The company employs the whole person with all their emotions, both good and bad. Marketplace Ministries of Dallas works with over 175 companies, furnishing chaplains for counseling, hospital visits, marriage and many services to their employees and families.

Father's Inspiration

The legendary film maker, Cecil B. deMille, says it was his father's influence that inspired him to go into the motion picture industry. *"We had to agree to rub his head so that he would read us Old Testament Bible stories before we went to bed...so soothed and relaxed that he would forget the hour and go on reading extra chapters to us as we sat intently around his chair.*

I have no doubt that my father's vivid reading planted in my impressionable mind a reverence and respect for the Bible, perhaps even a sense of dramatic values which in subsequent years was to turn me to the Great Book for themes to thrill motion picture audiences."

Cecil said that he had always been aware that the Bible was the perpetual "best seller" of all books, so he produced the movies The Ten Commandments, The King of Kings, The Sign of the Cross, and The Crusades. He once said, *"I've been in Hollywood since 1913, during which time actors, actresses, directors and producers have passed in seemingly endless procession, some befriended by destiny, others lost in oblivion. In a maelstrom like Hollywood there are many reasons for failure and unhappiness. I believe the chief among these is the failure to realize that the purpose of this life is understanding of the spirit and not worship before the calf of gold."* It is too bad that Cecil isn't around today to tell some of our present movie producers his story.

Love Has Different Degrees

Sensual - physical attraction, touch, look, smell, sexual
Respectful - authority, want to serve, recognition
Emotional - feelings, caring, sensitivity, appeal
Rational - decision to, ought to, want to, desire to
Agape - God's spirit flowing through a person, the strongest and most pure love, and as stated in I Corinthians

Family First

Mary Kay continues that, *"Our company was founded on our belief in The Golden Rule. We believe in treating people fairly, as we want to be treated ourselves. We apply this basic belief to every decision we make.*

In accordance with The Golden Rule, we strive to provide opportunities for women to achieve their maximum potential. We tell all of our consultants and directors that God and their family come before our company — and whenever they experience a conflict, the company should be put in third place."

> *"Put others before yourself, and you can become a leader among men."*

Returning Respect

"When it was time for me to step down from the day-to-day operations from the company I built from bankruptcy to $150 million in sales, says Jim Miller, CEO of BT Office Products, *"I refused to sell just to the highest bidder who would typically cut a third of our people and overhead so we became an instant plus to their bottom line. My people have respected my authority and leadership for all these years and I owe them something in return so I sold them a third of my stock to them at a very*

reasonable price and no one lost a job, yet our way of doing business keeps doing better. Our customer satisfaction index of 99.67 is a verification of that."

Biblical Inspiration

Samsonite Corporation was founded in 1910 by Jessie Shwayder with his life savings of $3,500 and a firm conviction to The Golden Rule. *"Do unto others as you would have them do unto you was the only way to do business,"* says Jessie, who felt that strong luggage — luggage as strong as Samson in the Bible, was his key advantage over the competition. Samson was what he initially named his products but later changed to Samsonite. Each new employee was given a marble plaque with a reminder of The Golden Rule.

Jessie believed God had entrusted him with the talents, resources, vision and capability to produce such a product, so he wanted to honor **His Heavenly Father** by sharing his principles with his employees, customers and suppliers.

Family Blessing

In 1979, Julius Erving, the famous NBA basketball player, sustained an injury that kept him out half the season. He said *"Somehow I got a chance to put things in perspective. We had a family reunion of 300 people on a three day weekend. We traced our history and I learned of a strong Christian influence, which I had not known before. One uncle told me that two generations before I was born my family put a blessing on me. They asked the Lord to bless me.*

I had to pursue this. As my uncle counseled me he said he had always been praying for me. His counsel put things in perspective and I was touched. I consecrated a relationship with Christ and it brought peace to my life and a destiny I had not known. It brought our family together to understand our purposes."

> *"America was founded on faith, so businesses had enough faith to take risks. Ongoing success is a result of using His principles."*

Father's Love

As Richard Kughn plodded home one day from school he found a cast off Lionel train engine. He took it home and later that night showed it to his dad. His dad took it apart and cleaned it and showed his son how it was put together. That was the beginning of a lasting relationship which influenced his life.

He claimed his dad had a God-given understanding of how to treat him with respect and develop a relationship that through the years became more than father and son but more like partners. He grew up, graduated from college, and was employed by a major corporation before leaving to start his own company. After a number of years of success he attended a train collectors show. A friend said, *"Dick, why don't you buy the Lionel Toy Train Company? I heard the company was for sale."* He laughed and dismissed the idea but couldn't get it out of his mind. After months of study his friends and associates had advised him not to buy the company. But as he prayed and pondered his decision he knew that God could see far deeper into things than he could.

"In listening for direction, and seeking the Lord's guidance, I thought of dad and me and what assembling and operating my train had meant to us. And soon after that I came across a picture of an old Lionel ad. It showed a youngster and his father on their knees amid a train layout, with the legend, 'Keep young with your boy and he will grow older with you.'

That picture made me think of the wide gap that seems to exist between children and parents nowadays. So I bought the company."

> *"The best way to forget your own problems is to help someone solve his."*

Over Ninety

Tony Campolo refers to a survey he conducted of people over 90 years old who were asked what three things might they do differently if they could live their life over again? These are the three things that were most common:

1. Take more risks — be open, let other people in.
2. Reflect more — avoid saying "just as soon as I get this done."
3. Do things that are eternal — things that live on beyond earth.

This is sound advice for all of us under 90. Before it is too late to influence and thank a boss, or counsel with an employee, we need to focus on the truths that bring each of us in tune with His eternal purpose of mutual respect and honor.

THE MORAL OF THE STORIES:

1. Honor those who brought you here whether they have loved you or not. God has a purpose for those he has placed in our paths and lives. Our role is to love one another, be forgiving and not hold on to bitterness and resentment. Seeking His love can overcome the past and bring back the sweet memories of the best of times for eternity.
2. Look to your employer with respect and honor, even if they have not treated you the way you would like. Pray for them. Share with them and be a part of each others' extended family.
3. Be a better parent. Spend time, share values, get into the Bible and fellowship with your spouse, kids and parents. Our purpose is relationships, not toys or big accomplishments.
4. Share with your employees and peers life changing and eternal truths. They may never get them anywhere else.
5. Show respect to father, mother or boss. Surprise them with a recognition event. Remind them of their outstanding qualities, contributions and appreciate results.
6. Pray for them, learn to love them.
7. The number one place that character and truth is taught or failed to be taught is in the home by parents. It's the cornerstone for the direction of our society. Day care can't teach the same values that mom and dad can.

Business Success

The greatest factor in the ongoing success of business and careers is based on the ability to follow the creation and moral truths of The Ten Commandments (also known as The Golden Rule) in their effort to "love" (care, empathy, service, and fulfilling the needs) of employees, customers, suppliers, vendors, community, and finally (not first) stockholders.

You ask, how then can "sin" businesses such as pornography publishers, drug dealers, and alcohol companies be successful? These companies also do their best to try to love or entice their potential customers who seek to "quench" the hurt in their heart. God loves the sinner (we all are sinners) but hates the sin. God is hoping the sinner will turn from his ways before he leaves the earth.

We Are Family By Design

Movement To And From His Truths

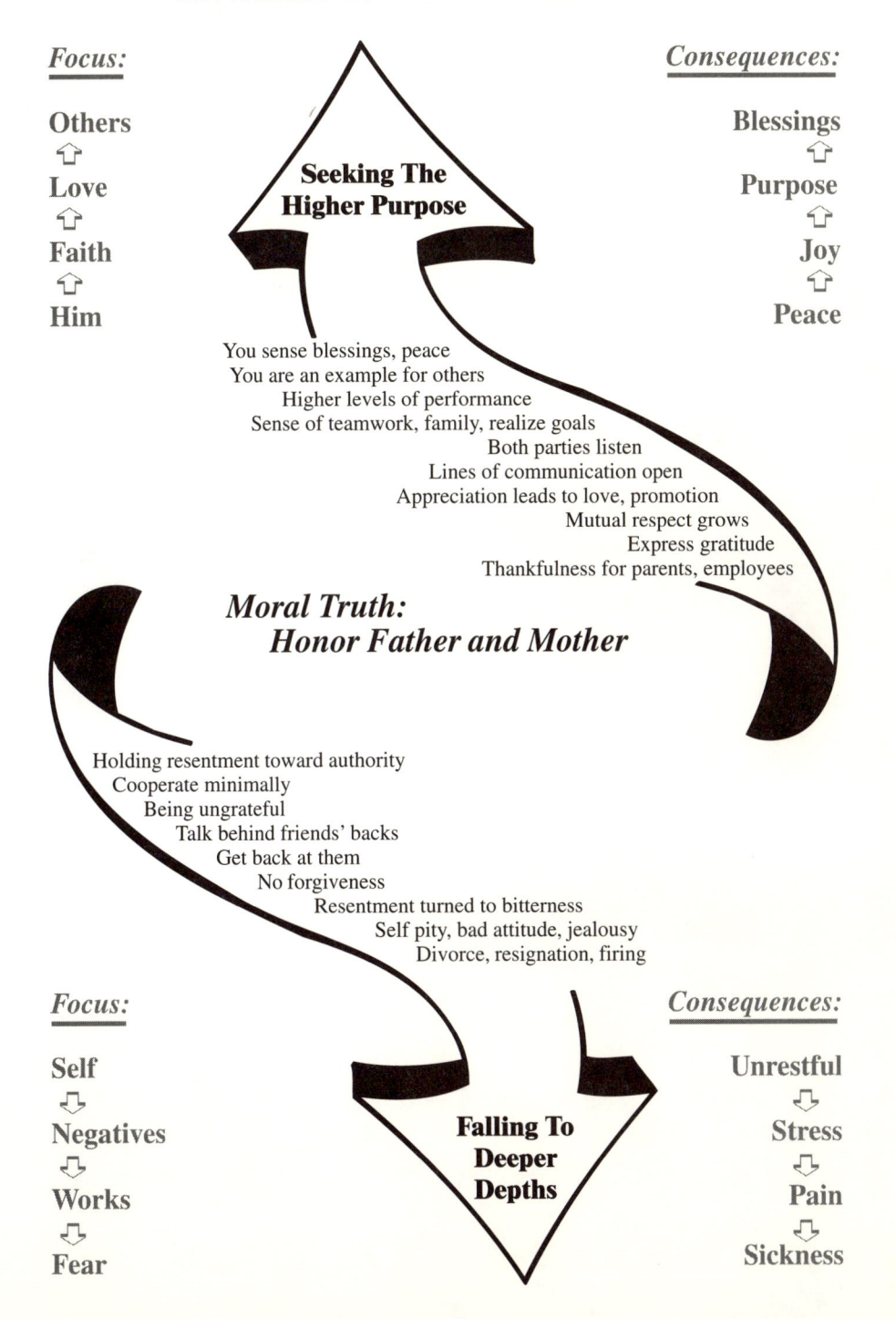

Focus:

Others
⇧
Love
⇧
Faith
⇧
Him

Consequences:

Blessings
⇧
Purpose
⇧
Joy
⇧
Peace

Seeking The Higher Purpose

You sense blessings, peace
You are an example for others
Higher levels of performance
Sense of teamwork, family, realize goals
Both parties listen
Lines of communication open
Appreciation leads to love, promotion
Mutual respect grows
Express gratitude
Thankfulness for parents, employees

Moral Truth:
Honor Father and Mother

Holding resentment toward authority
Cooperate minimally
Being ungrateful
Talk behind friends' backs
Get back at them
No forgiveness
Resentment turned to bitterness
Self pity, bad attitude, jealousy
Divorce, resignation, firing

Focus:

Self
⇩
Negatives
⇩
Works
⇩
Fear

Falling To Deeper Depths

Consequences:

Unrestful
⇩
Stress
⇩
Pain
⇩
Sickness

LIFE IS A GIFT TO CHERISH

Moral Truth: *Do not murder*

Character Quality: *But forgive and value life*

Hate or Forgiveness?

Adolph Coors, IV, faced probably the greatest tragedy that any of us could face, especially at just 14 years old. His father, who ran the Colorado brewery founded by his great grandfather, was kidnapped and murdered, shot several times in the back, and his body was found seven months later near Denver.

For seventeen years he lived with hate, anger and resentment for the man who murdered his father. While his mother never recovered, it seemed to have put Adolph's early years into a series of events that ended in frustration. The burden of caring for the family name and false expectations was very heavy, while he spent only a limited time in the family business.

Finally one day his life changed dramatically. He became a committed Christian. Total love and peace flooded him. He cried like a baby. All of the pain and hurt trapped inside of him seemed to rush out with tears.

His life changed as he grew in his Christian walk. Yet one burden seemed still to be there...the resentment toward the man who murdered his father. Through the persistence of a friend he visited the prison where the man was incarcerated.

His father's killer refused to see him. So he wrote him a letter saying, *"I ask for your forgiveness for the hatred I have had for you for seventeen* years and I forgive you for what you have done to me and my family." He visited twice more but never was face-to-face with his father's murderer.

However, on the last trip another inmate spoke with him and said, *"He got the letter, and it touched him. Your letter has also gone from cell to cell throughout the entire prison. You will never realize how great an impact this has had on the prisoners here, Mr. Coors."*

"The cure for crime is not in the electric chair, but in the high chair."

The Golden Rule

"I live by the Golden Rule," says Jim Moran, founder of Southeast Toyota, one of the largest automobile distributors in the world. *"I don't think respect or courtesy or kindness should be based on how much money a person has or what they can do for me. It does not matter whether you are the biggest customer or take out the trash — you deserve to be treated the way I want you to treat me."* Jim has had a colorful business experience and attributes his success to living by the Golden Rule.

Two Legends From the Same Branch

Jim Penney was a real pioneer in 1905. He broke away from the molds of the "wild west" mining towns. His Penney Idea set a new standard, still emulated today by many businesses. He was the first to call employees associates, share a third of the profits with the managers who were called partners, to price goods fairly rather than gouging, focused on customers' satisfaction and associate training and helping men and women develop their character.

Even though Sam Walton, founder of Wal-Mart, only worked for the J. C. Penney Company for a short time, he was fascinated with the Penney Idea. Sam was a master at learning from successful companies, but his frugal and conservative nature kept him from sharing company profits for many years. He later shared this in his book:

CHARACTER QUALITY

-Forgive and value life-

Unforgiveness hurts the person with the resentment far more than the person who we are bitter toward. This is why Jesus said to "love your enemy." By His design our heart can be severely damaged, which in time will create sickness or even death. Man deceives himself with the notion of getting revenge. God is the final judge in all matters. Forgiveness is not an option. Our job is to… focus on the central point of His truths which are about relationships… how to create a loving relationship with Him and our fellowman and how to have the discipline, respect, and consideration for one another. This is what pleases Him. At the same time, He wants to help us accomplish His purposes.

Business is not primarily about money, profits, stockholders, equity, "return on investment" or even whether we pay someone at or above the industry average. These things are secondary.

His measuring stick is spiritual. How much love, respect, dignity, empathy, or fairness do we share with our employees, family, friends and even adversaries. He did not create any "junk" and we all have handicaps...so we purposely need Him.

It is not our job to allow the emotions of deceit to dishonor or create disrespect between us. He has already forgiven us and paid the price. The least we can do is to forgive those who offend us and treat them with respect. Besides the family unit, business has the biggest obligations to fulfill His plan, "walking the truth" and being His example. "Vengeance is mine" says the Lord. After the law of the land, God will punish those who fail to repent. Besides the family unit, business has the biggest obligations to fulfill His plan, "walking the truth" and being His example.

How to get Rich... By the Book

"In the early days, we paid as little as we could get by with. The larger truth I failed to see was: the more you share profits with associates (employee salary, incentives, stock), the more profits will accrue to the company. Why? Because the managers treat associates in the way the associates will treat the customer...and if the associates treat customers well they will come back over and over and over and that is where the real profit lies, not in dragging first time strangers into the store for a one time purchase based upon splashy sales or expensive advertising."

THE PENNEY IDEA

To serve the public, as nearly as we can, to its complete satisfaction.

To expect for the service we render a fair remuneration and not all the profit the traffic will bear.

To do all in our power to pack the customer's dollar full of value, quality and satisfaction.

To continue to train ourselves and our associates so that the service we give will be more and more intelligently performed.

To improve constantly the human factor in our business.

To reward men and women in our organization through participation in what the business produces.

To test our every policy, method and act in this wise: "Does it square with what is right and just?"

Listen To Me

Maurice Mascarenhas, the late and enthusiastic Strategic Planning consultant, has shared this true story many times. Over the concerns for quality and competition, a very large company decided that it needed to get more employee involvement and set up a "suggestion system" to gather, review, implement and reward employees for their concepts which would save the company money and improve productivity. All the top executives seem to be pretty proud of the system as it started to work.

A year later at a dinner to recognize employees and give them cash bonuses, a long time hourly employee by the name of Herb Johnson was recognized. Herb's suggestion had saved the company nearly half a million dollars and the CEO was proud to give him a check for $5,000. Herb was asked to make a comment.

He said, *"I'm honored to receive this award and very pleased that the company had decided to recognize me for this contribution. I have been with the company for 14 years and made this same suggestion to my supervisor 12 years ago. He told me to button my lip, get to work and stop being so critical. All these years you have had my hands and now there may be hope that you will also get my heart and soul, as well."*

"Listening shows interest, respect and love, like the healing power of a prayer."

Bring Your Problems

Tom Watson and his son were credited for the significant growth and development of IBM over many years. He continually visited factories and spent hours talking with workers, inspiring the concept of "Management By Walking Around," so that many of them considered him their friend rather than the CEO.

One day an employee flew from Endicott to New York to see Watson. Doctors had told him that a younger brother had an incurable disease and would not live long. The distressed employee thought maybe Watson could do something that was beyond the medical resources of a small community. Within hours, the patient was under the care of a famous specialist in a top hospital, thus relieving his brother's anxiety. The employee then tried to apologize for perhaps overstepping himself, but Watson interrupted him, *"When I said bring your problems to me, I meant exactly that."*

"You cannot live a perfect day without doing something for someone who will never be able to repay you."
John Wooden

Policy Manuals

Robert Townsend, former President of Avis Rent-a-Car, in his updated book, <u>Further Up the Organization</u>, advocates: *"Don't bother with policy manuals. If they are general, they are useless. If they are specific, they are how-to- manuals — expensive to prepare and revise...if you have to have a policy manual, publish The Ten Commandments."*

A Short Course In Human Relations

The SIX most important words:
"I admit I made a mistake"

The FIVE most important words:
"You did a good job"

The FOUR most important words:
"What is your opinion?"

The THREE most important words:
"If you please"

The TWO most important words:
"Thank you" or "Forgive me"

The ONE most important word:
"We"

The LEAST most important word:
"I"

The Right Goal

As a partner in the New York City office of Ernst and Whinney, an international CPA firm, Homer Figler personally committed to his pastor that he would agree to read the Bible at least 15 minutes a day. The more he read, the more it seemed to change his life and perspective on things. Besides a personal impact, he could see how it directly affected business also. For example, he shared, *"One time I was having difficulty illustrating the importance of goal setting to a group of men and my Bible reading came to my rescue. I was able to show these executives an example of what happened to some people who were also working on a major project, people who did everything right except for one important element."*

Indeed, the ancient people described in the first nine verses of Genesis 11 had a common goal: to build a great city with a tower reaching to Heaven. They were in complete unity on the method, using fire hardened bricks for permanence. They committed themselves whole-heartedly to the task. But one thing was wrong; their goal. In effect, they were building the tower as a monument to themselves, putting themselves on a level with God. As a result, the tower was destroyed.

"If a goal — corporate, family or personal — is not morally right, something somewhere along the line is bound to break down. If a project is not fair to all those concerned, then those involved tend to let their private desires get in the way of the common goal. Communication breaks down, mistrust builds and instead of working together as a team, the group scatters — like the builders of the tower of Babel."

Divine Listening

After Jack Stack, CEO of Springfield Remanufacturing (SRC), and his team of executives were able to raise the capital to buy their company, they got production into high gear with a new sales effort. He felt pretty comfortable about their new direction. Things seemed to be working on all cylinders. Then one day walking down the hall he noticed a young man sweeping and said hello to him. The young man said, *"Did you know that 76% of our receivables are in trucking and every seven years the industry goes down? If the economy ever turns down, we will have problems."* I said, *"Thank you, Lord."*

"It just so happened that this young man had been a burned-out stockbroker and out of the pressure of it all decided to take a break and work for us. I was so taken by his comment and realized that he was 'right on' and went back to our management team and said, 'Do you realize that if we have an economic downturn we will be in trouble?' It was the turning point for SRC to diversify their business. Jack later said, *"That was a profound statement for our business and really changed the direction of our firm. I'm not sure everyone believes in divine intervention, but I do."*

*"The heart is the happiest
when it beats for others."*

Open Book Principles

American business executives seem to be constantly looking for the next "fix" or management trend that will be "the" answer to continual improvement and success in their business. Obviously the concepts of Empowerment, TQM, Re-Engineering, Value Added and Self-Directed Work Teams plus others will continue to help organizations be more effective and efficient and I believe with "right motives" aligned with God's truths…so that blessing will follow. But the "Open Book Management" concept, made famous and notable by Jack Stack and his team, can help businesses come even closer to adhering to the moral truths of The Ten Commandments if companies are willing to take the risks to implement them and "walk their talk."

Open Book Management focuses on four basic principles:
1. Sharing information and knowledge with everyone.
2. Teaching business literacy to everyone.
3. Sharing a stake in the outcomes.
4. Creating a company of entrepreneurs.

Open Book Management combines more of an opportunity of trust, relationships, team accomplishments, allows risks, treats people as family, where communication is demanded, and integrity and honesty are square one. I believe it reduces jealousy, internal competition, egotism, rumors and heightens morale. Overall, it is a better culture. Business needs to be both fun and profitable for all, and OBM can do nearly all of these things, if led by top executives with loving motives. OBM must operate in the **light** – where information is shared. God is love, truth and light. The "master of deceit" hides in darkness because he is exposed in light. He deceives executives into believing they should not trust employees with information. This creates problems - does not solve them.

*"We love customer complaints because we will
do our best to set things right."*
Clark Johnson, CEO of Pier One Imports

WHY DO PARTICIPATORY "PROFIT/QUALITY" IMPROVEMENT PROGRAMS WORK?

— They treat the individual with respect

— They communicate and give feedback

— They create family and team work

— They teach and build character

— They demonstrate and teach honesty

— They lessen jealousy through the use of numbers

WHY DON'T THEY WORK?

— Lack of <u>trust</u> of management's intentions by employees

— Doubt the ideas contributed will be used

— Jealousy   — Bitterness

— Resentment   — Poor communication (both ways)

*HIS PRINCIPLES WORK
FOR EVERYONE WHO USES THEM.*

*"Men Who Do Not Know Him But Follow His
Truths Will Be Blessed."*

Life and Death

When God created earth and man, he delegated to man and commanded, *"Take on my image — be fruitful and increase, fill and subdue and rule over the earth."* Two things he did not relinquish was control over the creation of life and death. Life is not only physical, but mental (soul) and spiritual. Heaven is for our soul and spirit.

Even with the blessings He provides us through our lives by way of His active involvement, one magnificent event brings Him more joy than any other: the creation of new life. God picks the color of eyes, personality, talents, and physical size — even the purpose for an individual's life. We may perform a sexual act but conception is His choice. Taking a life before birth is an **abomination** to Him and all that He has created. Someone would love any child, if it were given the chance to live.

Our will cannot take precedence over His. He gave us dominion over the earth but life and death are also spiritual and go beyond our responsibilities. Death by the hand of another man, outside the punishment for violation of laws and certain acts of war, is also an abomination to God. Life is eternal so His timing, just as in creation, is critical for the spiritual life of each person entering heaven or hell. At the same time, death of a loved one often has more impact and character growth on those left behind. God sees the big picture and has the ideal time for each of us.

MORAL OF THE STORIES:

1. This truth and character quality speaks to the heart of *"Loving your neighbor"* and The Golden Rule. Loving (caring, empathy, trust, kindness, openness and sincere desire to help) the employees, customers, suppliers, vendors, community, and finally, stockholders is what drives the ongoing success of a business. The Lord knew this when He gave Moses The Ten Commandments. It is part of His design, the culture, environment and human sensitivities that He built into us.

2. Good communication from the executive level down, as well as back up to the top management, is absolutely critical. As a family, a business must communicate honestly and lovingly. With poor or little feedback, we "miss the mark" and harm our business potential to be successful and the relationships that we attempt to establish with all parties.

3. We all make mistakes and "fall short" of the intent of a righteous God. However, He has forgiven us through His son. It is our responsibility to forgive those who have done wrong against us. If we do not, we will suffer the consequences within our spirit of frustration, bitterness, hate that can lead to stress, then physical illness, decline in business or other problems.

Life Is A Gift To Cherish

4. Our motive is key. If we want to accomplish something by manipulating people with circumstances or money for our self-centered gain, it runs in conflict with all the principles God has established. We should <u>not</u> be self-centered but God-centered and servants to our fellowman.

5. Many companies miss reaching their full potential because they focus on the wrong motives of making money, rather than ways to serve (love) the customers (all parties). Do this first and the money will follow as the reward, not as a purpose.

6. Downsizing for the personal gain of a few or to even benefit stockholders who do not work in the business is the wrong motive. Downsizing, if not handled properly, can "break the spirit" of a company. It is like breaking the momentum in achieving admirable goals. Downsizing because of a change in the market, and for the good of the majority, future health, goodwill and if in the customers' best interest can be the correct decision. How it is handled and how people are treated through that process with love, care and fairness is critical. The same is true for the employee who leaves the company. His resignation should be handled with respect, fairness and kindness.

7 Forgiveness is not an option for any of us. Others will offend or harm us. Unfortunately, some of us will do the same to others. We are all at different levels of character growth. Others don't mean to, but they reflect the hurt they feel inside and try to give it to us. Our job is to forgive and pray for them; otherwise, the bitterness we allow to live in our heart will harm us far more and get worse.

8. *"Do unto others as you would have them do unto you"* is The Golden Rule.

9. Operate your business in light, (God is light) not in darkness. Look at OBM and all programs which communicate trust and raise productivity and human achievement.

What Do We Worship?

Anger — is either acquired from a parent or through the seed words of bitterness, hate, or jealousy which take root in the spirit, build up and finally are released through yelling or violent acts. Anger is actually a defensive mode where we fight back from the fear of being hurt. The deep rooted bitterness or hate in the heart can only be cured through the healing power of the Word or prayer, which are spiritual. *Psychological counseling might help but seldom gets to the root of spiritual damage without the Word of God and prayer.*

Life Is A Gift To Cherish

Movement To And From His Truths

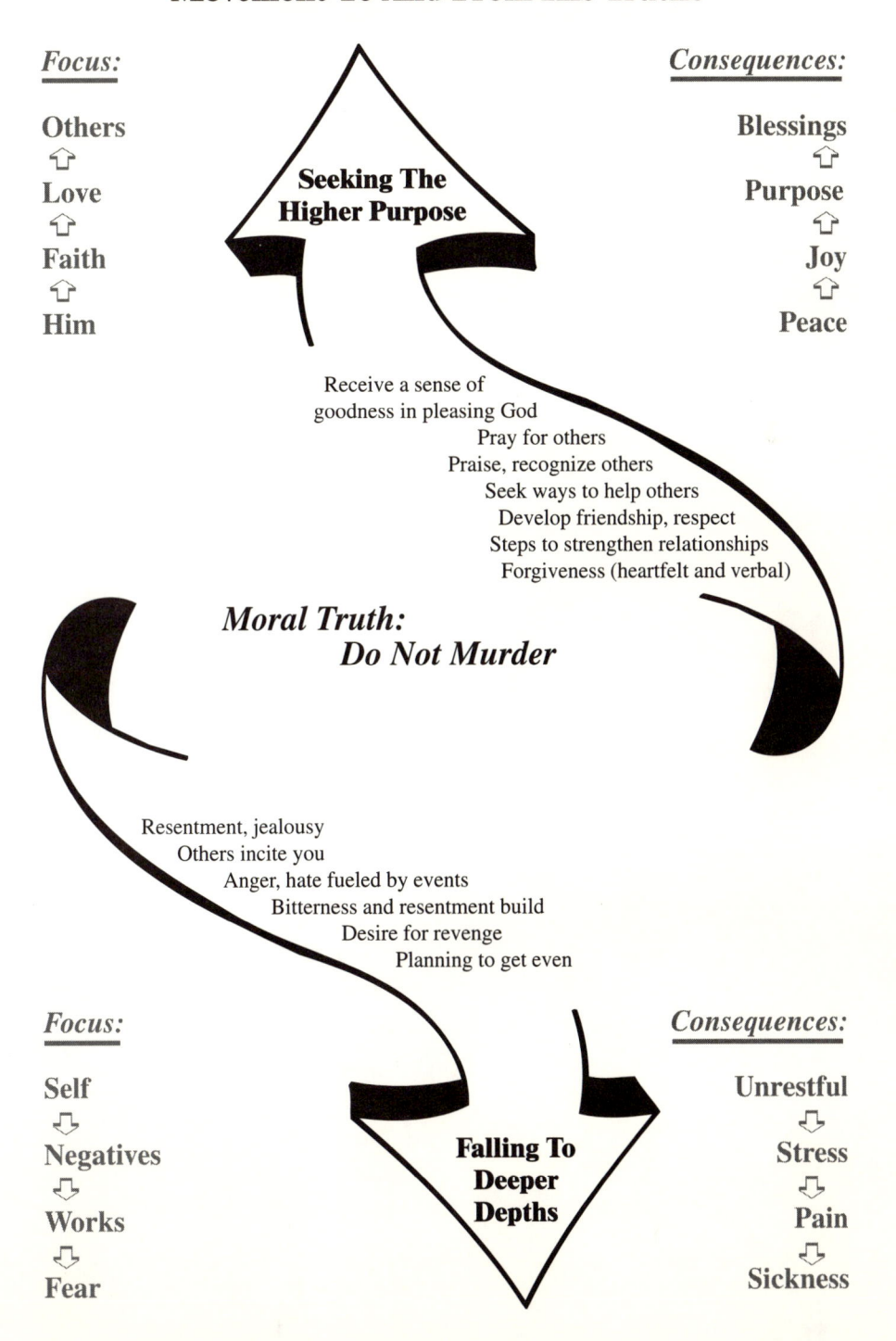

Focus:

Others
⇧
Love
⇧
Faith
⇧
Him

Consequences:

Blessings
⇧
Purpose
⇧
Joy
⇧
Peace

Seeking The Higher Purpose

Receive a sense of
goodness in pleasing God
Pray for others
Praise, recognize others
Seek ways to help others
Develop friendship, respect
Steps to strengthen relationships
Forgiveness (heartfelt and verbal)

Moral Truth:
Do Not Murder

Resentment, jealousy
Others incite you
Anger, hate fueled by events
Bitterness and resentment build
Desire for revenge
Planning to get even

Focus:

Self
⇩
Negatives
⇩
Works
⇩
Fear

Falling To Deeper Depths

Consequences:

Unrestful
⇩
Stress
⇩
Pain
⇩
Sickness

WELL DONE FAITHFUL SERVANT

Moral Truth: *Do not commit adultery*

Character Quality: *But be faithful and loyal*

Evil Turned Good

Lee Ezell was born and raised near Philadelphia by a mother and alcoholic father. At a Billy Graham Crusade she made a commitment to Christ. After graduating from high school she was bound and determined to seek a new life. At 18, she left home and moved to Northern California. After work on the first day in her first job, she was raped by another employee.

That night is horrible in her mind but she dusted herself off. In those days there was no place to turn for rape counseling and she certainly did not want to go to the police, but instead she "bawled her eyes out," and sensed a guilt she could not shake. Months later she went to her doctor because of feeling sick and he told her she was pregnant. She said, *"That can't be."* Being upset and distraught, she moved to southern California and happened to attend a church where she struck up a friendship with an older couple. Bible verse, Psalm 139 inspired her to reject abortion. The couple took her into their home until the baby was born. She did not believe that she could raise a young child as a teenager with no husband, so she gave the baby up for adoption the night it was born.

She had a number of up and down experiences but ten years later finally married a wonderful man who had two children of his own. She

CHARACTER QUALITY

-Be faithful and loyal-

Adultery is not only sexual but the violation of the personal integrity, relationship or covenant (emotional or physical) with another person or group. Violations of relationships occur between employer and employee, customers and others, far too often, as well. It is caused by the deceitful image that pleasure or personal gain is more important than principle. It is the false belief that self-discipline, commitment, faithfulness and integrity went out in the 1950's. The media image says you have to get all the "gusto" while you can.

Senator Bob Packwood was a great supporter of women's rights and abortion. Yet, at the same time he was an adulterer who violated the relationships of many women and purposely took advantage of his position. He may be one of the most shameful examples of a public figure who committed to serve the very group he violated.

By His truths, God is warning us that wrong acts draw negative consequences — perhaps not today, but eventually we pay the price here on earth or in the hereafter.

told him about the rape and child and he could relate because of similar losses in his life.

Years later she received a phone call. The voice on the other end said, *"Hello, my name is Julie. You've never met me but I'm your daughter and you are a grandmother."* Julie's adopted parents had raised her as a Christian.

In the anxiety to meet Julie face-to-face, Lee's husband talked to Julie's husband to tell him that she was conceived in rape. At first it was hard for her to accept but she later would ask her mother, *"Have you ever seen this scripture in Psalm 139:13-16 'You knit me together in my mother's womb, all the days ordained for me were written in Your book before one of them came to be.' "If this is true then God wanted me to be born."*

Lee was not only a successful wife and mother but a well sought after public speaker. She said, *"God does not cause evil but has a way of taking tragedy and turning it into a blessing. I found my missing piece and I believe others can too."* Both Lee and Julie have written a book, <u>The Missing Piece</u>, and have been on all the national talk shows and shared their message of hope and encouragement with thousands of people.

Unfaithfulness

In the 1960's America elected a President who had charm, looks, intelligence and confidence. While he was wealthy and thought to come from a good home, he seemed to pick up from his father some bad habits of "womanizing." He told an ambassador openly in front of others that he had to have sex at least every three days or he would get headaches. He openly discussed it with some reporters and propositioned women openly during his travels.

His affair with Marilyn Monroe was well documented and he finally broke it off after she pestered the White House staff who believed that she thought she had become the "second lady." At the time the media didn't report such stories or scandals because of their commitment to the public and to a nation with moral convictions.

But the Bible says that the sins of the father will affect generations. Certainly the Kennedy family has been greatly affected. There is a price to pay for unfaithfulness.

"The bridge you burn now may be the one you later have to cross."

Employee Loyalty

Compensation Design Group surveyed 500 companies nationwide to determine the loyalty of employees to their employer. When employees were asked whether they agreed that *"Loyalty between a company and its employees is said to be disappearing, do you agree?"* 79% said yes and 21% said no.

Next they asked the question, "Are you more or less loyal to your company than you were five years ago?" 29% said more and 61% percent said less.

The next question was "Do you feel your company is more loyal or less loyal to you than it was five years ago?" 22% said more and 78% said less.

When surveying different types of employee groups, the question was asked of each of them their plans to remain with their company. 20% of the hourly employees said they would, 25% of clerical, 30% of professional, 35% of middle managers, and 50% of executives. Again, businesses teach values by the commitments they keep or break. How those who are laid off or downsized are treated has a direct bearing on their image, reputation, integrity and sends a message louder than the rhetoric.

Sacrificing For the Few

World Life (fictitious name) was founded 60 years ago in one of our nation's insurance centers in the Midwest. The founder had made great sacrifices in developing and growing the business with a unique niche. Their sons grew up in the business, brought more education and innovation to the company, increasing the customer base throughout 25 states. As is normal in family run business, the third generation had not made the same sacrifices and did not have the same appreciation for what their fathers had built.

So by the 50th year and beyond, growth became slow - even flat. Rather than replace themselves with more capable management, they operated in "their way." While their fathers had contributed greatly to the community and vice versa, their sense of responsibility was more complacent.

Finally, the board said "Let's get our stock growing or cash out." Two years later they decided to sell the company because the profits weren't pushing up the stock value. They entertained three bids and finally accepted the highest bid. The buyer let go all the 1,000 employees and just folded World Life customers into their own home operation center in another city.

Well Done Faithful Servant

The community was outraged because of its effort to try and help the company. The employees were bitter as many had been employed 20-30 years and felt they weren't treated fairly. The two other bidders offered to keep the office open and keep the majority of employees. The officers took the less courageous way out, using the excuse that they were afraid some stockholder might sue them for accepting a lesser bid.

So rather than sharing some of the economic benefits with loyal employees and community, they chose to maximize their own personal returns.

A Great Place To Work

Robert Levering wrote the book, A Great Place to Work, after researching hundreds of companies and asking employees what they expected out of a great place to work. Here are the five common threads that most often were mentioned:

1. A friendly place to work.
2. Very little politics in the office.
3. Getting a fair shake from your employer.
4. An opportunity that is more than a job.
5. It seems just like a family.

Here are the words used most often by the employees:

1. Trust
2. Proud of their organization
3. Freedom
4. Treated fairly
5. Allowed to make mistakes

Morally Right versus Morally Wrong

Louisiana Pacific and Masonite are both manufacturers of press board siding for homes. Both companies have run into difficulty in terms of the life expectancy of the product. This has resulted in settlements with property owners, either individually or through a series of class action suits. Whether for the right reasons or not, they made the right moral decision.

On the other hand, the Manville Corporation which manufactured asbestos, ran into difficulties in the 1970's and 80's through the environmental discoveries of resultant poisoning of children. Rather than try to do right by its customers, it chose to do "right" by its stockholders. It filed for re-organization under Chapter Eleven bankruptcy laws. Federal Judge James H. Sarokin of Newark, New Jersey said that Manville "manipulated the judicial system so as to delay thousands of claimants and denied completely to some their day in court to present asbestos related injuries."

In 1982 the "Tylenol scare" cost Johnson & Johnson $250 million to yank all of its products off the shelves throughout the country. Their action was voluntary and swift. Their CEO claimed their decision was self-evident. They referred back to their corporate credo and philosophy of serving their customers first in making their decision. The correct moral and ethical decision by Johnson & Johnson has won national acclaim while Tylenol sales continue to grow each year.

The companies who choose the "short term win-lose" approach over what is morally right long term in serving their customers, commit adultery. These are the types of organizations and individuals which energize our legislators to write and pass more legislation to enforce the truths which are the foundation for our business ethics.

Finding an Answer

Charles Duke walked on the moon but his wife, Dottie, was in depression. She wanted love from Charlie and real fulfillment. After the space program, he and a partner started their own business to seek a new goal of making money. He was a workaholic and didn't provide the love she wanted. She searched, reasoned, struggled and even tried drugs to the point of near suicide. She saw no hope, yet they went to church every week. She had studied religions in college and was taught that they were all the same, that the key was just to love one another. So she didn't really believe in God.

By chance they went to a conference where a speaker shared why Jesus was different and that He answered prayer. Dottie decided that she would make a commitment to "try" Jesus. After He answered so many of her prayers she knew Christ was real.

But she struggled with forgiving Charlie for the things he had done to offend her. She had been putting her husband before God, and started to realize that only God could provide the love that she needed to be fulfilled. She realized her husband was not God.

Charlie was miserable in his business but through the change he saw in his wife and her prayers, he made his own commitment to the Lord. Their marriage was energized. Charlie said, *"it costs the government $450 million for me to walk on the moon for three days, and my walk with the Lord is free and will last a lifetime and beyond."*

This is the 90's

Recently, Disney, American Express and IBM pioneered the concept of providing health insurance benefits to partners of homosexual employees. Their commitment was most obviously based on two factors: economic and humanitarian. Valuable gay employees might resign now that they are so open which could produce an economic loss to the business. Secondly, in an effort to do "what is right" they believe everyone has rights and should be treated equally. On the surface, it appears to fit with God's moral laws of "loving your neighbor as yourself."

God appreciates that attitude and loves the homosexual as much as he loves anyone. However, homosexuality is about adultery and living in deceit. Same sex partners don't reproduce or begin a family unit by God's standard. Homosexuality is an emotional and spiritual problem psychologists can't correct. Only through God's grace can it be healed and there are many examples of it being done every day.

With a media attitude that adultery has no relevance because this is the 90's many major corporations are "too smart," "too much in-control" themselves to turn to a loving God to be involved to help them or their employees. The solution is spiritual counseling for these employees.

There is always a long-term consequence for "missing the mark" of His truths. If not economic, there is a greater potential of creating internal morale problems of jealousy.

Truth For Both Good and Evil

How can a loving God allow people to be financially successful selling pornography or drugs?

1. His truths work for all of us. If we sell pornography or drugs we are showing a love for the customer, filling their needs. Unfortunately, they are emotionally sick people, worshipping false idols of lust or addiction, leading to more sin. The business then takes advantage of the customer's weakness.

2. He does not see the financial return as Godly success—only as a measure of exchange. Our world wrongfully looks at wealth as success.

3. God wants to heal these people. He does not look at the pornography or drug dealer as worse sinners than those who lie to their boss or spouse or steal from the office. He wants all of us to repent, give up our ways and come to Him.

4. If the pornography or drug dealers do not repent or face punishment from the local authorities, then they will face the vengeance of God here on earth or in the next life.

*"Kindness is the oil that takes
the friction out of life."*

Foregoing Profits

Jack Eckerd, the founder of the multibillion dollar drugstore chain, became a spiritual Christian at the age of 70. He always considered himself a good man and attended church regularly, but his commitment changed his life as well as his motives. People said he was more at peace with himself and showed a "greater love in his heart."

His commitment brought to light something that he had totally ignored. He urged his Board and got their commitment to drop the pornography literature that they sold in 1,700 stores. They lost several million dollars in sales as a result of that action, but that did not stop him. Jack wrote to the president of other drug chains and urged them to do the same. As a result, seven drug chains and one national convenience store chain did the same thing.

The National Coalition Against Pornography would like for Congress to pass a law prohibiting businesses from selling pornography. Whether that happens or not, there is a higher law of morality calling us to do the right thing, not just for ourselves, but for our children and because of the pain inflicted through the perpetuation of sexual lust. At the same time, it is a heart warming example of how a CEO's moral decisions can influence so many lives.

"Decisions can take you out of God's will but never out of His reach."

THE MORAL OF THE STORIES:

1. Our relationships with other people are not to be forsaken. Life's relationships are about win-win, not win-lose. "What goes around, comes around," but most important is mutual respect and a love-based attitude that serves the will of our Creator, our fellowman over our self-centered needs. Life and business are team sports and the best players are willing to sacrifice themselves for the team.

2. We each need to look seriously at our personal and corporate decisions with a vision to the future. Will our decision adversely affect the health of the business and the relationship we have with all our customer groups? How would we like to be treated? The short term and least expensive way is not always a long-term win-win.

3. Are we loyal to our existing customers or always chasing new ones at a higher cost, better deal? Peter Drucker says, *"a business has a 1 in 16 chance of doing business with a new customer, a 1 in 4 chance of doing business with a former customer, and a 1 in 2 chance of doing more business with an existing customer."*

4. Are we spending enough time with our spouse and loved ones, instead of adulterizing our relationship because of our own personal wants, habits or the chasing of "success"?
5. Treat fairly the employees we have to let go and give them a good chance to find a new job.
6. When you resign, do it with integrity, appreciation and good will. Be a good example to others. The golden rule is good personal and corporate policy.
7. Treat those in relationship with you better than their expectations and you will be an example that others will emulate.

What Do We Worship?

Lust — for power, possessions, or sexual release are the most common. Sexual desire for a man is a craving and crying out for love. Men, more than women, express love through the sexual act. Sexual lust is a way to fill a spiritual void and hurt that becomes such a passion through mental pictures; that is how pornography, suggestive TV, commercials and clubs perpetuate the problem and stir up cravings.

Well Done Faithful Servant

Movement To And From His Truths

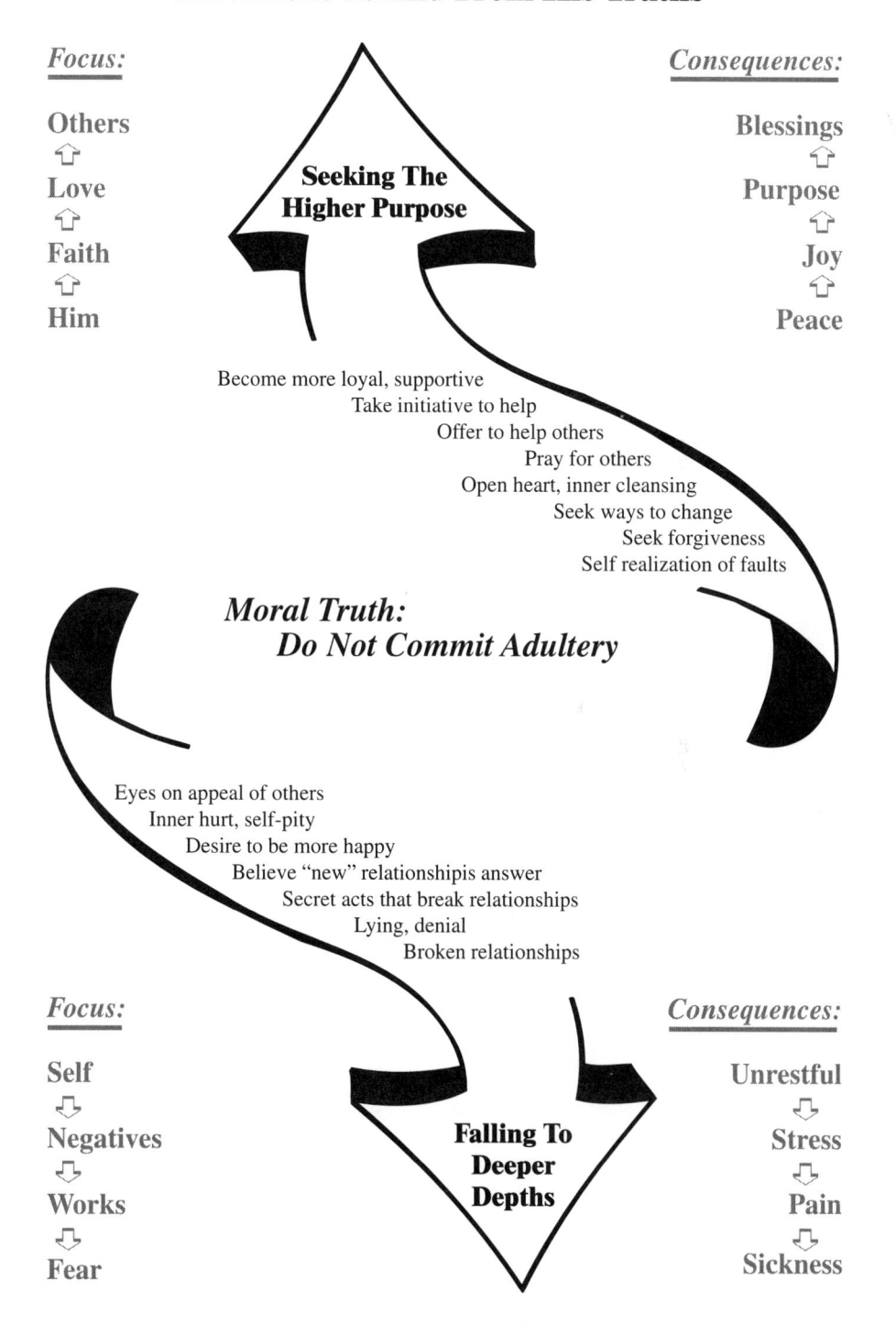

Focus:

Others
⇧
Love
⇧
Faith
⇧
Him

Seeking The Higher Purpose

Consequences:

Blessings
⇧
Purpose
⇧
Joy
⇧
Peace

Become more loyal, supportive
Take initiative to help
Offer to help others
Pray for others
Open heart, inner cleansing
Seek ways to change
Seek forgiveness
Self realization of faults

Moral Truth:
Do Not Commit Adultery

Eyes on appeal of others
Inner hurt, self-pity
Desire to be more happy
Believe "new" relationshipis answer
Secret acts that break relationships
Lying, denial
Broken relationships

Focus:

Self
⇩
Negatives
⇩
Works
⇩
Fear

Falling To Deeper Depths

Consequences:

Unrestful
⇩
Stress
⇩
Pain
⇩
Sickness

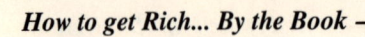

GIVING TOUCHES BOTH HEARTS

Moral Truth: *Do not steal*

Character Quality: *But give to others*

To Whom Much is Given

John D. Rockefeller, Sr. drove himself hard to be successful in business. At the age of 33, he had made his first million dollars. By dedicating every waking moment to his work, at 43, he controlled the biggest business in the world. By the age of 53 he had become the richest man on earth, the world's only billionaire.

For his achievement, however, he bartered his own happiness and health. He developed alopecia, a condition in which not only the hair on the head drops out but also most of the hair from the eyelashes and eyebrows. One biographer said he looked like a mummy. His weekly income was a million dollars, but his digestion was so bad he could eat only crackers and milk.

Newspapers ridiculed him as an industrial pirate and men that worked for him in the oil fields hung him in effigy. Body guards watched him day and night. Yet, he found little peace or happiness in the wealth that he had accumulated. He couldn't sleep and enjoyed very few things.

At 53 he was a frail man and newspaper writers had already written his obituary. One night he came to a spiritual and eternal realization that his wealth would do him no good in his life beyond...that money must not be hoarded but shared for the benefit of others. The next morning he got up and established the Rockefeller Foundation, which probably has had the greatest philanthropic impact on medicine in eliminating hookworm, providing Penicillin, and saving millions from the death of malaria, tuberculosis, diphtheria and many other diseases.

No one expected John D. Rockefeller to live past his 53rd birthday but after that night his health started to turn dramatically. He died at age 98 with the understanding, *"To whom much is given, much is required."* Rockefeller was a Christian and giver who recognized that he had a God-given talent for making money, but this experience caused him to realize that He wants us to give in proportion to what we receive.

CHARACTER QUALITY

- Give To Others -

In a simplistic way, stealing money and possessions are self-centered acts. Surveys have concluded that it costs the average American $200 a year in increased prices to cover the economic losses businesses suffer from retail theft alone.

Many Americans have a giving heart and understand the principle of "give and it is given unto you." The American Association of Fund Raisers in 1995 estimated that Americans give $144 billion a year to various charities, of which 45% goes to religious organizations. But the additional giving represents billions more through time, compassion and caring that comes from the heart...yet in countries where the government supports churches or charities with tax money, resentment is created.

The message comes through over and over again, do not be self-centered but be centered toward giving and helping others. As we give, our hearts are touched and we benefit...then the receiver's heart is warmed and a natural desire to give back continues the cycle. Even as we give the customer what he wants, he gives us his loyalty with the potential to be a customer for life. Money and the truth is to give first with no expected return - don't wait for others to give to you.

Milking Us

Stew Leonard's dairy store in Norwalk, Connecticut was considered to be one of the great entrepreneurial successes and role models for American business in the mid 1980's. The family store was a unique experience with fresh produce, meats, dairy products (plus animated animals and things for kids). It was larger than the typical supermarket with 3 times the volume. People traveled for miles because of the quality and experience of his store. Tom Peters and others shared Stew's great success with business executives around the country. Even major corporations wanted to learn how and what principles were used to accomplish so much.

On a trip to St. Martin in the Caribbean, Stew and his family had some difficulty getting through customs with $75,000 in cash. There is a limit on how much cash the government will allow you to take out at any one time. Because of this incident, federal agents started doing some investigations and discovered that he had diverted more than $17 million from income tax. Leonard was ordered to repay the stolen tax money and fined $850,000. At 63 years of age he was sentenced to 52 months in federal prison. Hoarding wealth beyond our reasonable and future needs works against God's plan for your life and those you could touch. When truths are violated, negative consequences will eventually occur.

International Pirating

The Wall Street Journal recently reported on the pirating of American video and CD's by foreign firms. The losses to American firms are estimated at $1.8 billion from Chinese companies, $726 million from Russia, $515 million from Italy, $285 million from Mexico, $273 million from Brazil. Recent federal trade agreements with the Chinese have generated commitments that they will crack down on this activity. I believe *"Is it the Lord's challenge to America to teach the moral truths (His ethics) to the rest of the world?"*

> *"You can't take your money with you, but you can send it on ahead."*

Dying Rich

John D. Rockefeller had an influence on many men, one of which was Andrew Carnegie, one of America's true industrial giants at the turn of the century. In 1889 Andrew Carnegie wrote an article in the North American Review in which he said, *"The man who dies rich, dies disgraced."* He also noted, *"The day is not far distant when the man who dies leaving behind millions of available wealth which was free for him to administer during life will pass away unwept, unhonored and unsung."*

Rockefeller wrote to Carnegie after reading the article, *"I wish that more men of wealth were doing as you are doing with your money, but be assured that your example will bear fruit."*

> *"A hundred times a day I remind myself that my life depends on the labors of other men, living and dead, and that I must exert myself to give in the measure as I have received."*
>
> **Albert Einstein**

The Calling Card

While in the Air Force, Aunt Della sent Wally Amos shoe boxes full of her delicious cookies. If there was anyone well liked on the military base in Korea, it was Wally Amos. When he returned home he went through periods of frustration in finding the right job. As he made sales calls he would take some of the cookies that he learned to make from Aunt Della, as his calling card. People loved them and urged him to start his own cookie company.

But Wally had more important things to do and his goal was to make it big time in the entertainment industry. Yet his marriage suffered and after thirteen years it ended in divorce. One day he pulled together his three sons in his 1960 Rambler and headed to the Grand Canyon. Little did he know that there he would see the beauty and splendor of God's work, drawing him spiritually back to the roots and heritage he had known as a young man in church.

As he returned home a new man with a new vision, he realized that his gift was in giving away cookies and pleasing people. This Godly inspiration led him to Famous Amos Cookie Shops, and later a world wide distribution company.

The Marketing Strategy With A Heart

Without fully understanding the "invisible economy" individuals and companies are using the giving principle and receiving back multiple returns. Giving to the United Way, to churches, to golf tournament charities, and homeless people are just some of the thousands of ways that we change the lives of others...but the motive needs to be unselfish.

The keys are the relationships, trust and love generated by giving first with no expected return. We have all seen men and women as executives of companies giving their time and money to important causes. There is a loving God rewarding that type of unselfish behavior in ways we don't even fathom.

Servant Leadership

Bill Pollard, of ServiceMaster, the multi-billion dollar public company, in his book, <u>The Soul of the Firm</u>, relates these comments: *"Socrates said that a person should first understand oneself as a means of making contributions to others." 'Know thyself' was his advice. Aristotle counseled his followers that to 'use one's talents to the utmost, one must have discretion and direction.' His advice was to 'control thyself.' But another great thinker changed history — and the hearts of people — with his unique approach to a meaningful life. 'Give thyself' were the spoken words of Jesus. In John 13 we read the story of how Jesus took a towel and a basin of water and washed the disciples' feet. In doing so, He taught his disciples that no leader is greater than the people he leads, and that even the humblest of tasks is worthy for a leader to do.*

Does this example fit in today's world, 2000 years later? There certainly is no scarcity of feet to wash, and towels are always available.

I suggest that the only limitation, if there is one, involves the ability of each of us as leaders to get on our hands and knees, to compromise our pride, to be involved, and to have compassion for those we serve."

Bill continues, *"For people to grow and develop within the firm, its leaders and managers must be prepared to serve as part of their leadership. Servant leadership is part of our ethic, and it means that leaders of our firm should never ask anyone to do anything they are not willing to do themselves. The leader exists, for the benefit of the firm, not the firm for the benefit of the leader. When we lead by serving, we are committed to be an example for others to follow, initiator for change and growth, and an activist for the future."*

*"We make a living by what we get...
We make a life by what we give."*

Giving Back

Having been left with his brother in an orphanage to be raised, Pat Kelly, the CEO of Physician Sales & Service (PSS), felt God had done him wrong by not giving him the opportunity to have a normal family life with a mother and father. After the age of 6, he only saw his father twice before he died. But Pat learned a lesson in the orphanage he may have never learned if he had had a normal family upbringing: He learned to share and get along with 60 other kids. This is a principle that dramatically impacted his entire leadership style...and helped to foster his company's innovation using Open Book Management concepts.

Having recently had the opportunity to visit another much larger orphanage, Boys Town, in Nebraska, Pat was deeply touched. His personal mission in life has changed because of this experience. His new goal is to give $100 million to the Virginia Home For Boys where he was raised.

Pat is just an example of many successful Americans who offer scholarships. Organizations like the Rotary, Kiwanis Foundations, Gold Tournament, Horatio Alger Association help needy young people with scholarships and opportunities they would have never dreamed of without them.

A Higher Calling

Reporters and writers are still asking Bill McCartney why he would give up a very successful college football career to begin a movement known as "Promise Keepers" which shares the gospel with men in major stadiums across the country. In just six years they have gone from a handful of men to well over a million attending their weekend conferences. Their ministry continues to explode and gross income alone this year will be over 140 million dollars.

Reporters say, *"You must have had a great marketing strategy. Who did you learn from? How did you see or predict this would happen?"* Repeatedly McCartney says, *"This is not me. It is not one man. It is not a group of men. It is a movement of the Spirit of God. I am merely giving my will to His calling with hundreds of men and organizers because it is so fulfilling to us and pleasing to Him. As we give to Him, he gives back to us with a sense of deep love, joy and commitment to purpose."*

> *"Those who bring sunshine to the lives of others cannot keep it from themselves."*

THE MORAL OF THE STORIES:

1. One of our highest callings is in giving and not taking. God pours out abundant blessings on those who give first with the motive of loving one another. For those with a Godly motive, they see depth in the phrase, *"It is in giving that we receive."*

2. To rob, steal, or take from another individual is selfishness. Some might feel they gain something with a temporary advantage in a short term way. But ultimately it comes back to harm our inner being and spirit through a sense of guilt, uneasiness, anxiety or even through hate.

3. Even if we are not reprimanded, accused or convicted over an unlawful act, we lose anyway. If we don't suffer the consequences or seek forgiveness here on earth, we will in the next life.

4. Personal volunteering, heartfelt giving is about "sowing and reaping." It affects us in this way:
   — Fosters relationships between people.
   — Touches the heart of the giver.
   — Touches the heart of the receiver.
   — The receiver senses more responsibility to use the gift wisely.
   — The receiver senses a desire to give back.
   — The cycle grows and touches more hearts.
   — People grow.
   — God is working in their hearts.
5. When the giving is <u>nonpersonal</u> (through taxation and given by a government for welfare, foreign aid, education, etc.), it becomes entitlement and eventually is resented. A dependency is created. Human initiative is dampened. The nonpersonal and lack of heart-felt giving dilutes the impact of God's truth working on individual lives. The potential for blessings are limited and the growth cycles reduced.
6. Love your neighbor as yourself (but not their money or possessions).

What Do We Worship?

Greed — money is important and necessary, but it is the love of money which hurts the human spirit. It becomes a craving or passion that becomes a sign of self-worth for many individuals. Without it they consider themselves failures and measure the work of others by it. At the same time, it creates an imbalance in a person's life because their idol can destroy a marriage, family, friendship, or even a business. Money cannot buy anything eternal. God gives some people talent to create capital and wealth, just as he gives an athlete great ability, but if they live their life for this one master it can destroy them in the long run.

Many deprived executives in their youth have taken on the god of money as a way to overcome the hurt that remains in the "underdog mentality," while others catch the sickness from their parents' attitudes. God wants many of us to be successful financially, but He also wants us to give back more, not look at money as a god. Unless you want to be buried in your Cadillac, money will do you no good after your death.

Giving Touches Both Hearts

Movement To And From His Truths

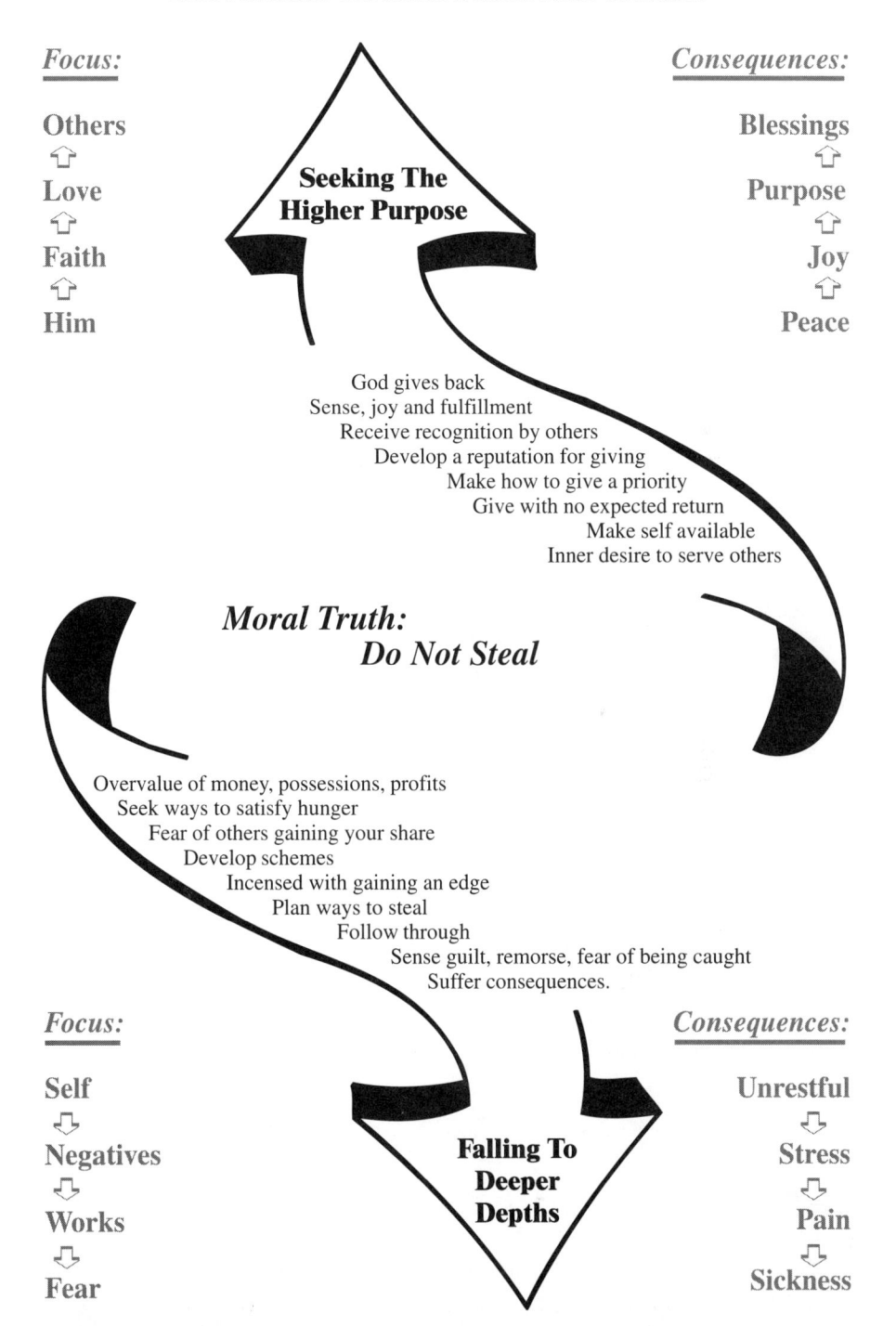

Focus:

Others
⇧
Love
⇧
Faith
⇧
Him

Seeking The Higher Purpose

Consequences:

Blessings
⇧
Purpose
⇧
Joy
⇧
Peace

God gives back
Sense, joy and fulfillment
Receive recognition by others
Develop a reputation for giving
Make how to give a priority
Give with no expected return
Make self available
Inner desire to serve others

Moral Truth: Do Not Steal

Overvalue of money, possessions, profits
Seek ways to satisfy hunger
Fear of others gaining your share
Develop schemes
Incensed with gaining an edge
Plan ways to steal
Follow through
Sense guilt, remorse, fear of being caught
Suffer consequences.

Focus:

Self
⇩
Negatives
⇩
Works
⇩
Fear

Falling To Deeper Depths

Consequences:

Unrestful
⇩
Stress
⇩
Pain
⇩
Sickness

151

How to get Rich... By the Book

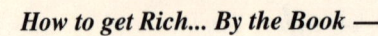

BETTER TO BE A POOR MAN, THAN A LIAR

Moral Truth: *Do not bear false witness*

Character Quality: *Earn respect and integrity through honesty*

Catch Me, If You Can

The story of Frank Abagnale is true. He ran away from home at age 16 over a broken heart; his parents had announced their divorce. Frank looked older than he actually was and impersonated a pilot for two years, passing bad checks as he went from airline to airline office. Next he impersonated a medical doctor in Atlanta for over a year. In Baton Rouge he passed the bar exam (on the third try), became a lawyer and was the Assistant Attorney General for nearly a year and a half.

Then he moved to Brigham Young University to impersonate a professor before a series of other escapades until he was finally caught in France at 28 years old. He had passed over $2.5 million in bad checks and was wanted in 13 countries.

He spent time in four different prisons until years later the FBI came to him with an offer to write procedures and policies for securing business systems from white collar crime in exchange for a commuted sentence. As a free man he began a normal life with family, and his own business, helping companies and corporations deal with all of these issues. He stresses to every audience he touches that he made mistakes that he really regrets. When he left home he gave up any chance of having a half-way normal life and he would love to relive his teenage years.

CHARACTER QUALITY

*-Earn respect and
integrity through honesty-*

In 1883 Abe Lincoln was postmaster in New Salem, Illinois until the position was abolished. Years later while a struggling attorney, a government official visited his Springfield office asking for the receipts of $18 which the government had never bothered to collect from the day the Post Office was closed. Lincoln asked the man to wait in his office while he went into his boarding room and brought back a blue sock with silver and copper coins and receipts (the exact sum and identical coins) and poured it out on the table for the government official.

Nothing destroys credibility, creates doubt or puts people on guard faster than someone realizing or suspecting that someone has lied to them.

The tone and culture established by management has to carry the message to their people of what is right or wrong or their success can be threatened everyday.

Our Creator did not design the body, soul and spirit to carry lies, bitterness or arrogance, to name a few. If an individual has any type of grounding in His truth, the spiritual guilt or mental anguish will lead to sickness, frustration or fear. Given long enough, the system will break down. "Coming clean" and forgiveness are critical before it leads to the authorities.

Impure Juice

Beech-Nut lost $5 million on sales of $62 million in 1981 and management was under pressure to turn the business around. Buying more expensive apple juice would have worsened the deficit because apple juice was a component in 30% of Beech-Nut sales.

Top executives in the firm decided to make a strategic decision that would be "penny-wise and pound-foolish." In November, 1987,

Beech-Nut Nutrition Corporation, the second largest producer of baby food, pled guilty to 215 felony counts for selling adulterated "bogus" apple food products from 1991 to 1993. Managers thought they were acting shrewdly but the costs to the company and to the owners proved to be anything but harmless or shrewd.

> *"The most valuable gift you can give another is a good example."*

A National Disgrace

Mark Twain is credited with saying *"If you tell the truth, you don't have to remember anything."* It is too bad that Richard Nixon did not know Mark Twain. He might have saved all of us from the national disgrace of Watergate. Power, fame, money and "success" have a tendency to breed egotism in many people. It is with egotism that we lose sight of reality and take on the "invincible" attitude. We can seem to get along successfully with a few white lies until the big one comes along that trips us flat on our face.

If Richard Nixon had been humble enough to admit to the American people that he and his people had made a significant mistake and apologized in an up front and timely manner, the whole incident would have blown over within two or three months, and everyone would have gotten back to business. Richard Nixon might have been considered one of the best Presidents in our history.

Egotism Causes Forgetfulness

John Wilson, a highly recognized CEO in the Midwest, achieved national notoriety a few years ago. He was interviewed by a well known business newspaper and asked to reveal the secrets of his successful marketing strategy. Flattered, he laid out his strategy and described how he created the system and implemented it.

As the article appeared, a friend of Bill Aronson, a top marketing consultant called him and said, *"Isn't that your material that appeared in the business newspaper?"* It just so happened that this marketing consultant had shared his concept and strategy three years earlier with an association audience that John had attended. Unfortunately John forgot where the information had come from and took it as his own creation but all materials were copyrighted. No credit was given to Bill and his organization. The issue was settled out of court but it cost John significant money for his learning curve.

We All Pay

Price fixing, check fraud schemes, falsifying information for government contracts, savings and loan schemes, insider trading...these are just examples of things that cost businesses and customers billions of dollars each year. The message starts at the top, in the board rooms, in company policies and business ethics principles that are shared or not shared with employees. Also, the legal costs to prosecute the criminals responsible is staggering, is a waste of our money and an abomination to our creator's truths and warnings.

> *"The level of motivation in an organization can never rise above the level of trust."*
> **Clark Johnson**

Lying For Employment

Bennett Brown, CEO of Enterprise Bank, a healthy young entrepreneurial bank growing at a rapid pace, shares an incident of a few years ago when he needed a new vice-president for a newly created department. By chance he interviewed an outstanding candidate with significant bank experience. Rather than move quickly in the hiring process as he usually did, he decided to use an outside testing and screening company to help him in his decision. They discovered some discrepancies in the candidate's background and when confronting him, he admitted that he had "decked" the CEO of the last bank that he had worked for because of his anger with him. This is the reason that he left his last employer off his resume. Don Walker, former FBI agent, reports that it is estimated that 35% of all candidates falsify information about their college on the resumes. This merely points to the fact that business needs to do its part in exemplifying and teaching the importance of honesty to its people, otherwise we are part of the problem and not the solution.

"People are hired for what they know and fired for who they are."

Ed Ryan

Loving Employees Serve Better

The American Society for Quality Control reported a study indicating why customers are lost.

Here are their findings:

Perceived Indifference by company employees	68%
Product Dissatisfaction	14%
Competition	9%
Influenced by friends	5%
Move	3%
Death	1%
Total	100%

The Used Car Salesman

There is something unusual about Dave Schwartz from Los Angeles. He has sold used cars most of his life, but his philosophy seems to be different. *"If something was wrong with a car I was selling, I would rather fix it, and if I couldn't fix it I would tell the prospect up front. If a battery was weak he would know it. If the car used a lot of oil he wouldn't have to drive 100 miles to find out."*

"People would tell me, Dave, you're nuts. Everybody knows you can't make money in the used car business that way." Well for years Dave proved them wrong and then something unusual happened. A young lady wanted to buy a used car because she had a short assignment in L.A. and wanted something cheap that would just last for the time she was there. But after they discussed it, he decided to rent her the car, saving her money and allowing him to make more money. This helped Dave's concern about doing what is right. This way she would only have the car a short time and have less chance of it having problems.

He discovered a new business concept which became so successful that others wanted to franchise the concept. Today there are several hundred "Rent-a-Wreck" agencies in the United States and Australia. Here is what Dave tells a prospective franchisee. *"If money is your only goal, then forget it. I believe that in any enterprise, if you make money your god, then the business will never be really successful. For then you are never satisfied; you've put the cart before the horse."*

He continues, *"But if a person enjoys filling needs and making people happy, then there is no end to his success and he doesn't have to worry about money."* It was all put into one sentence two thousand years ago by Jesus Christ when he said: *"Whatsoever you would have others do unto you, do unto them."* (Matthew 7:12).

"There's a world of difference between truth and facts. Facts can obscure the truth."
              Maya Angelou

Taking a Stand

Larry Rosen has been a highly successful furniture retailer who was convicted to develop a code of morals and ethics for people. Later he became increasingly concerned about selling their largest line of furniture.

Larry shared, *"We were telling the customers what the manufacturer told us to say, that they are the best in the industry. I knew it wasn't true and it bothered me more and more until finally one day in prayer the Lord worked on my heart. I knew it was time to give up that line of furniture."* Once he did it his sales dropped by 75%, but Larry's conscience was clean. He was at peace over his decision and ready to move on to successfully rebuild his business.

Carl Terzian heads up the largest independent public relations firm in Los Angeles and has many well known clients. What's different about Carl is that in his nearly forty years of business he has never asked a client for a signed contract. Everything continues to be on a handshake. Clients can leave whenever they like. But this allows him to do the same...to ask a client to leave when he feels his ethics or business practices are not fair or honest.

"Some executives say to me, 'But, Carl, you know business is business,' and I say to them, 'That is a cop-out. You can't forget your fellowman or His values that we all need to live by." Carl says that *"The more companies fail to teach their employees and hold them accountable to what is right and wrong, the more our nation will have to pass laws to try to legislate the individual actions of people and their companies. This is where businesses are failing."*

> *"To educate a person in the mind and not in morals is to educate a menace to society."*
> **Theodore Roosevelt**

Recall Programs

Very few business executives would put Ralph Nader at the top of their list of favorites. But what his consumer movement did was to force businesses to stand behind their products and deliver what they promised. Recall programs are now a way of life but they are right. It is a shame companies could not have done them voluntarily before having to succumb to government intervention or threats.

International Integrity

It is estimated that bribes are commonplace in 60% of the countries around the world, especially in underdeveloped countries. The smarter American firms bidding for these contracts refuse to give bribes. Once a company starts to pay bribes, their reputation is known, and they are continually caught in having to keep up with the game. At the same time, these government officials will look for someone else's bribe, making it more competitive and difficult to keep a government contract.

There is increasing national attention over products imported to the United States using child labor in underdeveloped countries for very low wages. The wages paid in some of these countries are extremely fair or even above the average employment wage in those nations. What's happening is that this attention demonstrates to these underdeveloped countries that America through its free press and many businesses will teach our predominant value system: an ethic derived from The Ten Commandments. In the long run that should help the world's economies come closer to parity - a quality we need to achieve in a world marketplace and serve God's plan.

"If you don't stand for something you'll fall for anything!"

Your Word

Ken Wessner was a pioneer with ServiceMaster. During his early years of starting contract cleaning in health care businesses, they lacked the national credibility or reputation because of their size and the health of their balance sheet.

After making a presentation to a hospital board they asked for Ken's financial statement. A few board members said that they could not use them because their balance sheet was weak. A respected board member who had known Ken and his integrity spoke up and said, *"I know Ken Wessner and when he gives his word, he will do the job!"* Without that meaningful relationship of trust, ServiceMaster would have not had its first sale in this industry, which turned into a $2 billion management services division employing more than 150,000 people.

Corporate Honesty

Honesty has to start with internal communication as well as complimentary external communication. Performance appraisals, terminations, meeting customer expectations, and communicating with employees timely, forthrightness, sharing both the good news and the bad, is absolutely critical but too often neglected by executives. Most executives will make the statement to employees, *"I don't want any surprises, so if you have any bad news share it with me ahead of time."* The same courtesy should be extended to the employees by top management.

Sharing numbers with employees consistently, given that they are trained to interpret and understand their meaning, is an excellent tool. It can increase trust, reduce prejudicial comments about performance or productivity, and increase a sense of ownership and responsibility to contribute and perform at a higher level. This is why real quality programs and Open Book Management are effective tools for business.

THE MORAL OF THE STORIES:

1. The **poison** that can kill good moral works of an individual or company is dishonesty. Honesty may be the highest regarded moral ethic in the American business world.

2. When company executives or employees say one thing, do another or do nothing, without explanation, their honesty is questioned. Their reputation becomes such that people aren't sure when to believe them, as in the story of Peter and the Wolf. We all need to "walk our talk."

3. No communication to employees over critical events, performance or actions, as well as poor communication, borders on dishonesty.

4. Lying is an attempt to control the circumstances of a situation for one's own personal gain. This focuses back on pride and self-centered behavior. Again, God is calling us to be God-centered and centered on helping other people...forget yourself and do what is right for others.

5. The future of business is more dependent upon the morals your employees bring to your organization and the character you teach and demonstrate to them. Any employee can kill or rape your business without firing a shot or taking a dime. How? By just dumping key data on a few discs and giving them to people who have bad motives and desire to harm you or your business.

What Do We Worship?

Gluttony/Addictions — This usually starts with the development of a habit in seeking pleasure because of a spiritual emptiness that only He can fulfill. As depression or frustration gets worse, the dependency gets stronger. The addiction provides the temporary high for relief. It becomes our "fix" (or god). It is what we worship and can't live without. Since it is spiritually rooted it is impossible for any one individual to totally overcome this by his own willpower. Changing to a dependency on God has the greatest chance for a turnaround. Besides drugs, alcohol, smoking, and food, there are a number of other addictions we might seek, i.e., work, TV, being a sports fanatic, or even simple things like golf, tennis or other sports. Aside from drugs, alcohol and smoking, these other activities do not have to be addictive if we just keep them in proper balance, rather than letting them become a release that we worship and can't live without.

Better To Be A Poor Man, Than A Liar

Some Ways Employers Can Love Employees

Love is	Filter	Company Programs/Actions
Patient	*Are*	Strategic planning process
Not angry		Involvement
		Lay out time table
Convicting		Accountable
Tough *		Measure
		TQM
Kind	*Company*	Smile, act caring, concerned
		Rewards
		Recognize
		Terminates with respect, help
		Involve family or associates
Not boastful		Watches the tongue
Not evil		No false idols
Not rude	*Leaders*	Act and teach respect, management
Truthful		Communicate bad as well as good news
Not self seeking		Humble toward others
Not proud		Recognizes people
Not boastful		Gives credit to deserving
Forgiving		Policy - we learn from mistakes, take risks, no reprimands
Protects	*Walking*	Good financing package for stability
		Defends legally
Trusts		Work teams
		Delegates authority
		Back-up people
Hopes	*Their*	Communication
		Share vision, dreams often
		Research for future
Preserves	*Talk?*	Profit sharing, ESOP
		401K, bonus, new job opportunities, create new companies

* Tough is added to I Corinthians

How to get Rich... By the Book

Movement To And From His Truths

Focus:

Others
⇧
Love
⇧
Faith
⇧
Him

Seeking The Higher Purpose

Consequences:

Blessings
⇧
Purpose
⇧
Joy
⇧
Peace

New customers, friends, seek you
You are sought as an expert
Customers, friends, respect you
You are promoted
People rely on you
People seek your advice
People trust you
Honesty is your character

Moral Truth: Do Not Bear False Witness

Desire to get ahead over integrity
Tell "white lies" to gain advantage
No one seems to notice or care
You scheme for promotion, money
Follow through with lies
Lying becomes second nature
People suspect you, talk about you
You are confronted and lie again
Guilt and stress build
You are caught and fired

Focus:

Self
⇩
Negatives
⇩
Works
⇩
Fear

Falling To Deeper Depths

Consequences:

Unrestful
⇩
Stress
⇩
Pain
⇩
Sickness

14

DIVERSITY IS A STRENGTH

Moral Truth: *Do not covet*

Character Quality: *Appreciate and encourage others*

Trouble Ahead

"*I'll never forget the day Branch Rickey, former President of the Brooklyn Dodgers, asked me to join his baseball organization. I would be the first Negro to play in organized baseball — that is, if I were good enough to make the grade,*" said Jackie Robinson. Meeting in his office *"was the never-to-be forgotten day when our Marines landed on the soil of Japan, August 29, 1945. From behind his desk the big, powerful, bushy browed Branch Rickey, who seemed a combination of father and boss, mapped out to me his daring strategy to break the color line in major league baseball."*

"*Mr. Rickey,*" I said, "*it sounds like a dream come true — not only for me but for my race. For seventy years there has been racial exclusion in big league baseball. There will be trouble ahead — for you, for me, for my people, and for baseball.*"

Rickey picked up on my words by saying *"That's the way it is with most trouble ahead in this world, Jackie — if we use the common sense and courage God gave us, but you have got to study the hazards and build wisely."* He continued, *"God is with us, Jackie."* *"You know your Bible. It's good, simple Christianity for us to face realities and to become what we are up against. You can't go out and preach and crusade and*

CHARACTER QUALITY

- Appreciate and encourage others-

To covet is based on self-centered emotions such as prejudice, jealousy, envy, and bitterness. From a spiritual vacuum we find comfort in our own "pity party," blaming others for our hurt. Pride and humbleness again are key. The Lord knew this would be a problem for us if we didn't sincerely work toward being appreciative and encouraging the differences between each of us.

If you were God how would you create people in the world? Would you create everyone the same and give them all the same talents? That would be boring for Him and ourselves. We would all want the same things and be even more apt to fight, disagree and be competitive. Or would you create each of us with talent equal to God? In that case He would have a big problem...He's the only one who has a right to be jealous and isn't looking for any more competition.

He created us all unequal so that He could have the joy of working through our lives as He is called upon and to see us grow and nurture just like a father or mother does with their own child. At the same time with different needs, we all need each other and can support each other because of our different talents. No question - He has a good design.

bust our heads against the wall. We have got to fight out our problems together with tact and common sense."

Jackie's first year was with the Montreal Royals Farm Club where pre-season exhibition games were canceled because of "mixed athletes." One of the critical things for Jackie to have to avoid was the "outbursts" of ball players over calls or incidents on the field. *"But I didn't dare lose this way. Many would have dubbed me a "hothead" and point to my outbursts as a reason why Negroes should not play in organized baseball. This is one of the hardest problems I had to face."* Montreal that year won the Junior World Series and Jackie won the batting title with a .349 average. *"On April 10, 1947 Branch Rickey made the announcement that gave me my greatest thrill. I joined the Brooklyn Dodgers and became the first Negro to compete in the Major Leagues. I prayed as I never had before."*

"Again I faced the same problems as opposing players drove a hard

grounder to the infield. When a player crossed first base his spikes bit painfully into my foot. Accident or deliberate, who could tell? But the first reaction of a competitive ball player is to double up his fists and lash out. I was blinding red. It took every bit of my discipline to bridle my temper. When my team mates rushed to my support in white hot anger, it gave me the warmest feeling I have ever felt. At that moment I belonged."

Can I Come Home?

Johnny Simmons was a young Vietnam soldier returning home and sent to Los Angeles before being discharged. He called his mother from a hotel and said, *"Mom, I'm back in the States and will be coming home soon."* He also said he had a friend he wanted to bring home with him, but the friend had been badly wounded and lost one eye, an arm and a leg. He asked whether that would be all right.

His mother's voice was hesitant, then she finally said okay, but only for a couple of weeks or less.

A few days later his mother got a call from the L.A. Police Department, reporting that her son was dead. He had jumped from the eighth story of a hotel window. She was told also that her son had only one arm, one leg and one eye.

*"To return evil for good is devilish...
To return good for good is neighborly...
To return good for evil is God like..."*

The Corporate Game

Karen Hanson's story is based on facts but changed slightly to illustrate a point. At 22, fresh out of college, Karen was hired by a Fortune 500 Company based in Chicago. She was smart, attractive, and aggressive. Within her first three years she was promoted five times and her vice-president counseled her a number of times about her future career with the company. He was her "champion" supporter and decided to give her a territory in a metropolitan area as a sales coordinator that was 26th out of all 28 territories.

He was criticized for giving somebody so young such a responsible position but most didn't think too much of it because the territory was considered "a loser." She had one hurdle, however. She had to be approved by the local manager and other staff.

In his interview with her, the manager questioned why she would want this position and told her that she would never make it because she was too young and attractive. After all the dust settled, the manager decided to give her a try.

Within nine months she had brought the territory from number 26 to number 6. At a corporate wide meeting she was recognized twice because of the great turnaround in her area. Many employees she left behind were jealous and created rumors and criticized the boss behind his back for his decision to promote her. The CEO questioned him as to why she had been promoted so quickly.

From on high, the corporate board decided it was time to cut costs and improve margins, to increase profitability and be able to get the "flat" stock to appreciate more rapidly. So the message came down to consolidate the sales territories with Karen's area combined with a previous male's area. Karen was asked to take a lesser position and in disgust, bitterness, hurt, and a series of broken promises, she resigned.

These kinds of stories can be found in most companies and represent the "company politics," internal conflicts, productivity problems and jealousies that exist. They damage morale and keep many companies from reaching their full potential.

> *"A critical spirit is like poison ivy...*
> *It only takes a little contact to spread poison."*

Tit-For-Tat

In another case, George Williams was hired from the outside to take over a department which was "misfiring." Within three months he had done an excellent job and seemed to be performing very well. Everyone seemed to be working as a team.

Diversity Is A Strength

Case I — How Resentment Builds

Resentment starts — "You are just trying to look good!"

Defensive, getting back — "You are just jealous because you are not as good!"

Spreading the word — "He's trying to make us look bad!"

The word spreads fast. — "Let's get back at him!"

More resentment is created, barriers are built, productivity hurt!

Case II — Resentment Overcome

Resentment starts

Sincere, forgiving and not defensive.

Spreading the good word

The word spreads fast.

Harmony, openness, caring are fostered. Productivity increases.

A new CEO was brought in and asked for performance reviews in light of salary increases proposed. Tom was George's direct supervisor and they always seemed to get along with one another. Tom made the typical mistake of focusing on two small problems with George on his face-to-face performance review rather than the big picture and overall evaluation, then laid out a very small raise for George. There was some bitterness and jealousy between the two that seemed to be covered over before.

George, like many people, was good at hiding his emotions and hurt but made a conscious decision that he would get revenge. He took immediate action. He called his former employer to determine whether they might have a job for him. Within two weeks he was gone. Tom, holding onto his resentment and pride, was not willing to apologize or make any effort to correct his mistakes and the CEO did not want to intervene and take away the responsibility he had given Tom.

The productivity of George's department went down and the expensive search to find another person began.

Message or Messenger?

Pricie Hanna of Scott Paper was promoted to the position of staff vice-president for corporate planning at age 32. Her boss said, *"It is a big job, Pricie, and a tough one, but based on your performance we are confident you can handle it."* Pricie was entering into a new era working with an all male group and thought to herself, maybe I'm the "token woman." But she was confident she could handle the job.

Six months later she was called on to make a significant proposal for direction of the company. She said, *"I launched into my presentation with some very significant recommendations and had barely finished when another vice-president, obviously anxious to have his say, presented his strong opposing views. As he spoke, I could see the other men nodding their heads in silent approval. In the ensuing debate, my efforts to reinstate my opinions fell on deaf ears. It seemed to me that the others had their minds made up ahead of time. A dreadful thought crossed my mind: Is it just my ideas or have these men rejected me?"*

"Personally, I was devastated. Time and time again, I was allowing myself to imagine all kinds of slights and ill will."

"At home one night in frustration I was reviewing corporate reports and finally tossed them on the floor as I felt the anguish of my position. I started thumbing through my Bible for wisdom, comfort or encouragement of some sort. I stumbled onto the Book of Daniel and saw that he had had similar experiences dealing with three different CEOs (kings) but had relied on his Heavenly Father to guide him through his difficulties. His strategy was simple enough. He just prayed three times a day."

I said, "If that can work for him, maybe it can work for me. The idea of praying anytime anywhere — even in the company of business associates — was inspiring. Through prayer God could be with me in a close intimate way whenever I felt alone or insecure or shy."

I concluded, "Lord, I have put you in charge of my home and now I have put you in charge of my job and my whole life. I felt better about myself, my colleagues and the challenges I faced. I got my eyes off myself and put them on Him. I moved from the "hot seat" to another promotion but this time God went with me."

"People who try to whittle you down are only trying to reduce you to their size."

Are you Dead?

Bill Cosby, in a speech to students at Howard University recently aired on C-Span, asked the question....Are you dead?

Dead people are waiting to get something. America is a bitter place for dead people. You are polluting the society if you are just sitting and complaining.

"If you don't want people to judge you, don't judge others....don't get stereotyped. Get pride in yourself and forget the easy stuff.

— Stop going to movies that are degrading.

— Disassociate yourself with stereotypes, when you don't want people to do it to you.

— Don't waste your money on bad music.

The fight is about progress. You have to have respect and pass it onto your siblings.

You want to hear the music, do the dance, but you have to pay the piper. You can only blame the person responsible and sometimes that is you. You can become our heroes."

Bill Cosby's comments were not just for "College Students" but for the "me" generation that has been bent on "picking their own values." They are part of the efforts that the media and others want to create in our own mind, that we don't want to offend anyone, rather than focusing on the eternal values which are the higher standard.

"If your heart is right, your mind will follow."

Hating the Boss

Laura Nash in her book, <u>Believers in Business,</u> tells the story of Andy, a Christian who was a supervisor in a manufacturing facility. Unfortunately he worked for a boss he did not respect. He said, *"I was preoccupied by the injustices I was witnessing and was angered that such behavior was producing bad results for the business."* Those types of feelings hurt Andy and he felt guilty. Even though he did not discredit them, he felt a sense of "hate" inside.

At his local church he was involved in a Bible Study group and shared his frustration with his pastor. The pastor asked him to share it confidentially with the other men to give him advice. Andy felt comfort knowing he was not the only one that had had these kinds of anxieties, but the group gave him good counsel as well.

Andy's conclusion was as a Christian he needed to use his faith and should start praying in love for his boss. That realization was transforming because it was very hard to hate someone you were praying for. Praying for someone is an act of compassion, love and concern. The net effect was a powerful change in his attitude toward his boss. Andy still did disagree with many of his decisions but he no longer was preoccupied with proving him wrong. He found the patience to say, *"The fate of my career and this man's are in God's hands, not mine."* Quite suddenly one day Andy was promoted over the other man, who was allowed to "retire."

"Every person should have a special cemetery lot in which to bury the faults of friends and loved ones."

Walking The Talk

University of Chicago Annual Survey, provided by Rob Lebow, "A Journey into the Heroic Environment," of over 10,000 employees conducted annually, asking "what they want from their employer?"

People Values

- Treat others with uncompromising truth.
- Lavish trust on your associates.
- Mentor unselfishly.
- Be receptive to new ideas, regardless of their origin.
- Take personal risks for the organization's sake.
- Give credit where it's due.
- Do not touch dishonest dollars.
- Put the interests of others before your own.

Notice how closely those align with The Ten Commandments.

Pray For One Another

Focus on the Family is an international ministry based in Colorado Springs founded by Dr. James Dobson who has a worldwide radio show by the same name. Dobson is also a famous author, while Focus on the Family has 52 ministries and over $100 million in annual donations.

If you were to visit their organization, you would see something that is unique from the internal operations of a typical business. Their

Diversity Is A Strength

organization's principal goal is to counsel with people and help them through milestones and difficulties. (Isn't that what every business is supposed to do in helping the customer grow and fill their needs?) Each week department staff meetings review personal as well as business goals while each staff member is encouraged to pray for one another. Yes, it may not be the very most efficient but neither is bickering or jealousy that occurs in most organizations. In using this method there is a better appreciation and understanding of differences and a compassion for one another. Often family concerns hinder personal productivity. You can sense a real difference in the commitment toward one another and caring for people.

No Comparison

"Don't look at somebody else's life or position and say I wish I could have that," says Joe Gibbs, former NFL coach. *"God has a plan and you are different. I realize now that God was molding me, building my character (during those times of defeat and frustration) and I needed to be made ready to be a head coach. The key is trust Him, that God will work in your favor."*

"He who throws dirt loses ground."

THE MORAL OF THE STORIES

1. While the poison of honesty can kill, the alcohol of coveting and its equivalents slows a business heart rate with the potential of slow death.

2. Company executives create the opportunities for people to covet, be jealous or envious of others. For example, they can create undue competition for promotion to the top positions in the company. This can create jealousy, bitterness, rumors and resignations. Recognition is good, but a matter of being in proper balance. Servant leadership, horizontal management, character training, team recognition and other

programs help to deal with this more constructively.

3. The bottom line is that coveting, jealousy, envy, bitterness, prejudice and hurt all create productivity within the organization and reduce the effectiveness of team work and potential profitability. This is the biggest area of waste in American business.

4. If we hold the words of bitterness, envy, jealousy, etc. within our heart, they turn into weeds, discomfort, lack of peace, pain and sickness. That is why God said *"Do not covet."* He knew how he built the emotional, physical, mental and spiritual part of our being. Rarely do any of us go around telling someone else that we "hate them" but when keeping the pain of that word in our heart, we suffer every time we see the person. We are the ones who suffer, rarely does the person who is hated. It hurts us far more than it hurts them.

5. The purpose of a business is to be a tool of God, building the character of each of us, learning to love, grow together toward His purposes and respectful of different roles, talents, stations and economic circumstances.

What Do We Worship?

Envy — is learned from parents and the deceit of others. Again it is a hiding place for a damaged heart. People find comfort in "pity parties," wallowing in the hurt they feel of being deprived, short-changed in life, so they become paralyzed in their dreams and desires to have what others have and allow bitterness to become resentment for others. It is fueled with gossip and breeds more jealousy and hurt.

Diversity Is A Strength

THE DOWNWARD CYCLE

Focused on department interests

Loyal to department concerns

Protective of department needs

Distrusting of "outsiders"

Influenced by rumors and false reports

Committed to erroneous conclusions

Makers of false accusations

Controlled by hidden/open conflict with other departments

Dedicated to internal competition

Drained by energy loss

Burned out by inefficiency

Hampered by lowered productivity/quality

Customer dissatisfaction

Revenue Loss

From Beyond
the Bottom Line

How to get Rich... By the Book

THE BODY OF THE COMPANY

**We are all created to take on His image.
Everything needs to work together for good to succeed long term.**

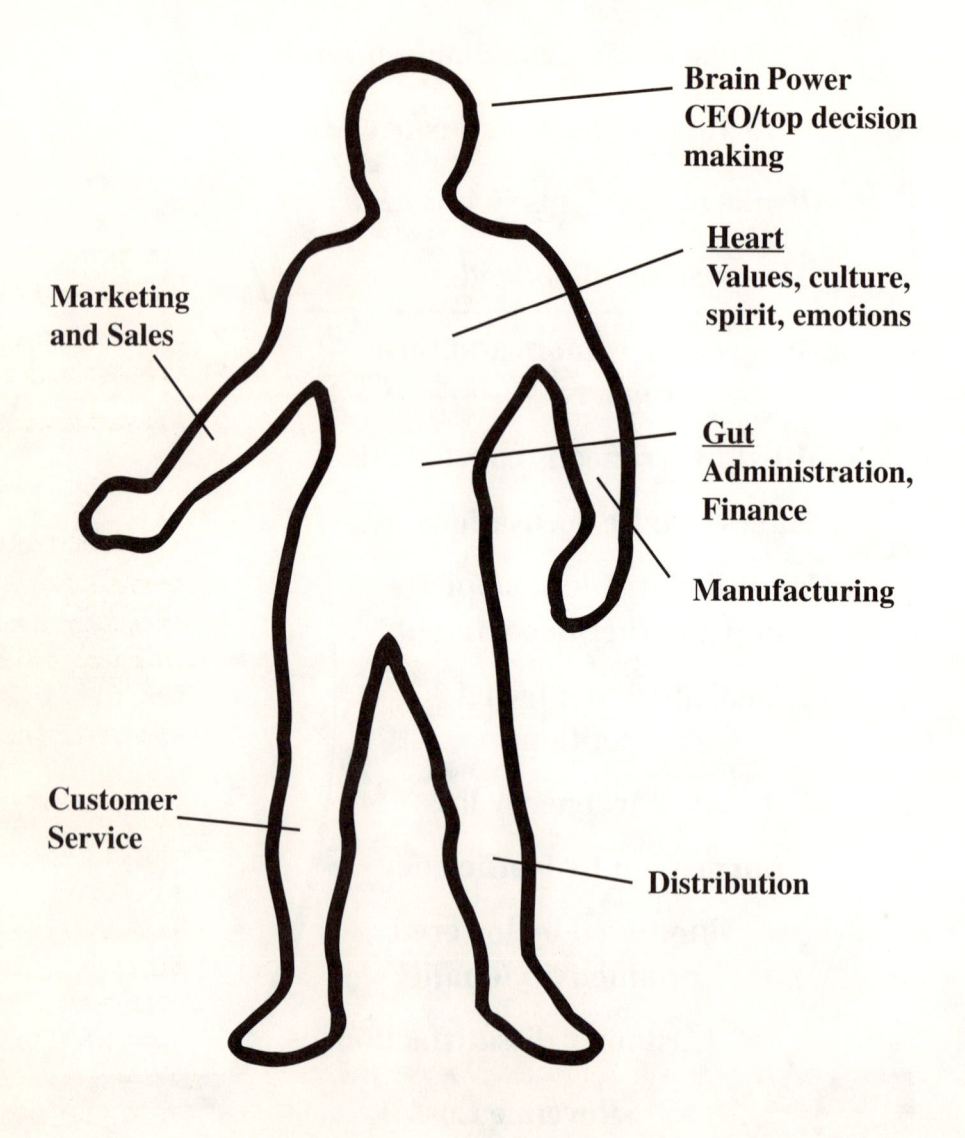

Brain Power
CEO/top decision making

Heart
Values, culture, spirit, emotions

Marketing and Sales

Gut
Administration, Finance

Manufacturing

Customer Service

Distribution

Every body part is different on purpose to function as a unit, as such all parts suffer if one part is hurt.

Diversity Is A Strength

Movement To And From His Truths

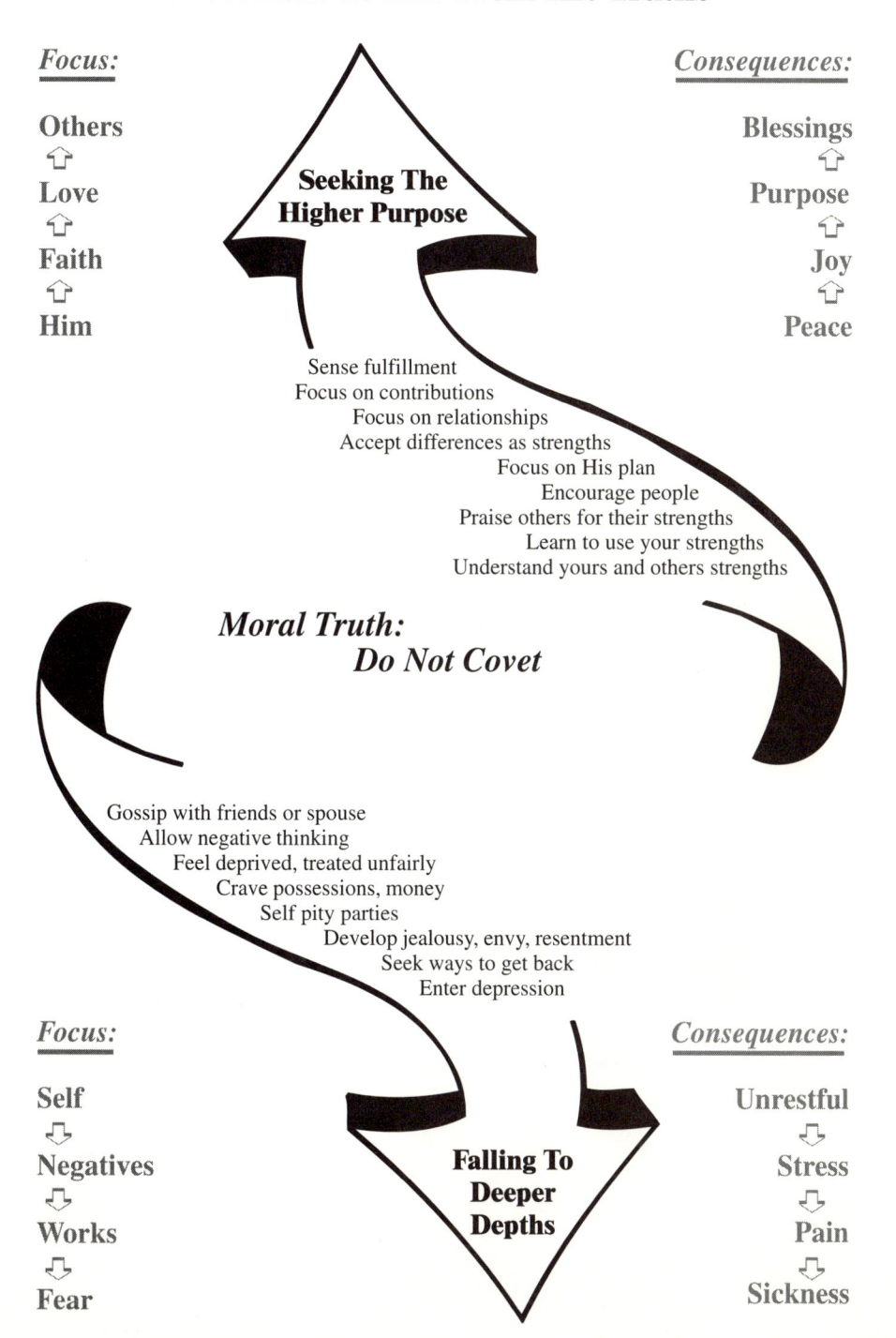

Focus:

Others
⇧
Love
⇧
Faith
⇧
Him

Seeking The Higher Purpose ⬆

Consequences:

Blessings
⇧
Purpose
⇧
Joy
⇧
Peace

Sense fulfillment
Focus on contributions
Focus on relationships
Accept differences as strengths
Focus on His plan
Encourage people
Praise others for their strengths
Learn to use your strengths
Understand yours and others strengths

Moral Truth:
Do Not Covet

Gossip with friends or spouse
Allow negative thinking
Feel deprived, treated unfairly
Crave possessions, money
Self pity parties
Develop jealousy, envy, resentment
Seek ways to get back
Enter depression

Focus:

Self
⇩
Negatives
⇩
Works
⇩
Fear

Falling To Deeper Depths ⬇

Consequences:

Unrestful
⇩
Stress
⇩
Pain
⇩
Sickness

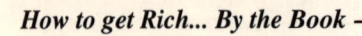

THE BOTTOM LINE

Self-Centered or God-Centered?

In the 1980's, J.C. Penney Company had to make some critical decisions about their future strategies for business. David F. Miller was President of J.C. Penney Stores and Catalogue and the decisions he and his team made set the company on a new course of growth and prosperity during a difficult retail era and even more competitive decades ahead. Having had the privilege of knowing Jim Penney personally, Miller became a lay speaker sharing Jim Penney's story with his church members a few years ago. He allows us the privilege to share his message with you.

"I would like to refer to this experience as Pastor's Appreciation Sunday. After listening to me, you will appreciate your pastor a lot more! On a serious note, each of us — in our lack of spiritual consciousness — gives ourself credit for what we term our "success" in life. Frank Sinatra's popular song, "I Did It My Way" has been a top hit for nearly two decades. Advertising slogans like "You owe it to yourself" are seen and heard everyday. We generally believe it.

Positioned against this view is the consistent admonishment from both the Old and New Testaments to seek first the kingdom of God and His righteousness — to pursue a spiritual consciousness. Thus we live our lives with an eternal struggle: Should our focus be God-centered or self-centered? Self-focus most often proves to be destructive. Experiences from the life of Mr. James Cash Penney can help us better understand how dangerous and defeating such thoughts can be.

Jim Penney spent his youth in the small farming town of Hamilton, Missouri. His father — whom he credits for his understanding of ethical business behavior — was a circuit-writing preacher during the latter half of the 19th century. He served the church without pay while providing for his family by farming. Their existence was austere, even harsh — devoid of any material excesses. Mr. Penney, however, recalls those days in his writings with great warmth and certainly deep respect.

Commerce seemed to come naturally to Jim, and at the age of 8 he began raising pigs as a source of income to help his family. He was resourceful and energetic — and the pig population grew rapidly. Unfortunately, as he writes, 'I was doomed to disappointment. The pig-pen is an unpleasant neighbor during the hot summer months — a fact that was brought to my attention by complaints received by my father.'

Jim's father made him sell the pigs, telling him that he should respect the rights of his neighbors and not profit at someone else's expense. The senior Mr. Penney quoted 'The Golden Rule' to young Jim as the basis for his decision. Jim respected his parents, and adopted their beliefs as he began a merchant career in the local dry goods store as a combination stock boy/junior clerk.

His hard work and dedication eventually led to other opportunities, specifically in Colorado. His effort there resulted in the opening of his own store in financial partnership with his two former employers. An unlikely spot was selected — the small mining town of Kemmerer, Wyoming. The store was opened in April of 1902 — thus, the beginning of the J.C. Penney Company.

Borrowing from his parents' teachings — and through his own talents and hard work — he was immediately successful. While he required the same hard work and cooperation from those who joined him in his dream of building a retail empire, he was quick to recognize the value of sharing — not only the financial rewards — but in giving those who worked with him the opportunity to become partners, just as his former employer had given him.

He used the term, "Associate," rather than "employee," and profit sharing became one of the fundamentals in the early growth of the business. He looked for and accepted as partners only those who shared his ideals and willingness to sacrifice. In short, Mr. Penney may have been the first practitioner of what we refer to today as a "real business partnership" — dedication, hard work, loyalty and singleness of purpose on the part of the worker, reciprocated by recognition, sharing, financial reward, and a high degree of security on the part of the employer.

Perhaps most importantly, in guiding the business, he insisted on ethical dealings. In fact, in the beginning his stores were known as "The Golden Rule Stores." So he prospered. By 1917, just 15 years after the opening of that first store in Kemmerer, Wyoming — the Penney Company was financially sound...a rapidly expanding chain of 175 stores.

In keeping with this extreme confidence in his partners, in 1970 Mr. Penney turned over the daily operations of the organization to a hand-picked, personally trained successor, Mr. Earl Sams. With Mr. Sams at the helm, Mr. Penney was free from day-to-day operations of the business.

He was in great demand as a speaker on his favorite subject — "Christian Principles of Business." He and his family traveled extensively, both at home and abroad. He was received world-wide by national leaders as a giant in retailing — an entrepreneur of enormous prestige. He co-founded "Foremost Dairies" to bring quality dairy products to the market at very competitive prices. You might say he was the original "off-price" retailer.

Like many other men of wealth during this period, he saw Florida as a promise of the future. Using some of his accumulated wealth, he purchased tens of thousands of acres of Central Florida farm land, with the idea of shipping produce to the big eastern cities. His dream was to relocate families to Florida, where they would train and become partners in farming. He would bring quality, fresh produce to millions — just as he had done with clothing, dry goods, and dairy products.

Grateful for the sacrifices of his parents, he built and dedicated in their memory a retirement community for ministers of all denominations. Even today, the town of "Penney Farms" in Northern Florida is regarded

---

Why is The J.C. Penney Company Still In Business?
After 90 years, is it because:
— they have good people? good products?
— they have good strategy and culture?
— they are flexible and adapt to change?
— or because God promises generations of blessings to a faithful founder?
— or all of the above?

as a model community, boasting one of the highest educational levels of any city in the United States.

Expanding his interest in Florida, he became a central figure in one of the largest land booms in American history. He accepted the position of Chairman of the board of City National Bank of Miami to lend his name to the enterprise, although he had no intentions of managing the daily affairs of the bank. So, as the 20's drew to a close, Jim Penney would smile with satisfaction. He seemed to have conquered the world, although he clearly had not overcome the world. He had "done it his way." Then came "Black Tuesday."

The week of October 26, 1929, the New York Stock Exchange lost 21% of its value that week. Over the next thirty months, the paper wealth of those who had invested in America's financial empire plummeted by 81%. The land boom in Florida took the most severe hit of all. City National Bank of Miami was closed — bankrupt. Mr. Penney's losses were heavy, but they represented a reasonably small portion of his total wealth.

His enormous holdings in the J.C. Penney Company, for the most part, were still intact. The company was being soundly managed by Mr. Sams and his partners. In fact, the chain was growing by absorbing other retailers as the depression took its toll.

Mr. Penney's name — and somehow his reputation — were inexorbitantly intertwined with the bank in Miami. Thousands of depositors had lost their entire savings, trusting in the bank whose principle director was James Cash Penney. His name was often associated with the disaster in the headlines of the local papers. They asked — How could it happen? When so many had lost all, how could Jim Penney still remain secure and — by any standard — extremely wealthy?

Those headlines devastated Mr. Penney. Unable to satisfy himself with a legal interpretation of his innocence, he borrowed millions against his Penney stock to keep the bank open — and also to continue supporting the J.C. Penney Foundation and his other philanthropic interests. As the stock market plummeted, he began to sell his Penney stock at now substantially reduced prices to cover these loans. The downward spiral continued, and in the end this once extremely rich man found his wealth totally depleted.

By 1931, the financial battle was over and James Cash Penney had lost. He was financially and emotionally broke — from king to pauper in *just a few years. Where had he gone wrong? What had he done to deserve this devastation? He searched in vain for answers, but they would not come. He sank even lower, and a physician friend — unable to help — finally recommended his sanitarium in Battle Creek, Michigan for rest and treatment.*

One night, while there, he became convinced that he would never see another day. He wrote a letter to his wife and children, asking for their forgiveness and understanding. After 57 years, he was certain he would depart this world in total defeat. He spent that night in tortured anguish, expecting to die, yet searching for some evidence — some sign — from his Creator that his life contained meaning.

Finally, the dawn came. He had survived the night, but only to face another dreaded day. In a weakened stupor, he wandered down the hall of the sanitarium — <u>totally</u> devoid of any self-confidence or pride of personal success. He was a lost soul in every respect. It was in this wretched, defeated condition that Mr. Penney began to find lasting answers to his life. Let me relate how he later described the experience:

I passed a parlor in the sanitarium and heard a choir singing, "God will take care of you." A few people had gathered in the religious meeting and I felt urged to enter. In great weariness of spirit, I listened to the hymns, to the scripture reading, and to the prayers. Then, a profound sense of inner release came over me. A heavy weight seemed to be lifted from my spirit. I was amazed at my change, and in the days that followed, I regained mental and bodily health. Perhaps the feeling of death that night was a symptom of a new beginning born in me.

In that small religious meeting, Mr. Penney recognized
- *that being honest and moral were not enough, God wanted his mind as well, "as a man thinketh, so is He."*
- *that he must first seek the kingdom of heaven, and that all things would be added thereto.*
- *that he had lost nothing of value, that he was a child of God.*
- *that wealth and power / not God — had been the motivating factors in his life.*
- *that J.C. Penney Company was not the product of James Cash Penney, but the infinite mind of God working through His child, Jim Penney.*

Mr. Penney left that institution a few days later, having rearranged his personal priorities. "Blessed are the poor in spirit, for theirs is the kingdom of God." How divine these words of the first beatitudes must have seemed to Jim Penney.

He had finally realized that it was "*the divine consciousness* within him that must be in charge of this life — the positive force that is available to all of us if we take the quiet time to listen. He vowed that what remained of his life would be given entirely to God. And so it was, for nearly 40 years, he used his influence, his skills, and his service in the application of Christian principles. He advised others to do the same, saying, those who have the greater part of their adult life before them should study with great earnestness the relation between Christ's two commandments — to love God and to love they neighbor as thyself."

At James Cash Penney's death, Dr. Norman Vincent Peale's eulogy said of him, "He became ever more humble, with a disarming wonderment about him that these great things could happen to him. His benefactions and good work shall ever bless his name." That was high praise for a man who forty years earlier faced a life of total defeat. From that night in Battle Creek, Jim Penney had a never ceasing commitment to follow the first commandment: "Love thy God with all thy heart, and with all thy soul and with all thy might."

His story is a lesson for all of us who are tempted to focus on ourselves as the power behind our accomplishments and our success. "Whosoever shall exalt himself shall be abased; and he that shall humble himself shall be exalted." (Matthew 23:12).

"None of His truths say to focus on yourself."

THE MORAL OF THE STORY:

1. God's truths are calling us to three principles of:
    A. Creation - taking personal initiative
    B. Spiritual - personal relationship with Him
    C. Moral - love our fellowman
 J. C. Penney grasped and implemented the creation and moral

truths. He thought he had all that God had planned for his life. Through humbleness, he discovered what he had not understood...God wanted a personal relationship, to love and be loved by Him. He wants the same from each of us. This is the secret to real richness in life.

2. Any manufacturer has limitation on the use of their product, i.e., an automobile may not be designed for the desert or towing a boat, or a suit is designed for summer wear rather than winter. All products have limits to their use, stamina and longevity.

> God is the manufacturer (designer and Creator) of each of our lives.

Our limitations are listed in the "owner's manual," the Bible. The more improper use or stress we place on our body, soul and spirit, the greater the chance for pain or breakdown of the parts. He doesn't have to "raise a finger" when we get out of our lane. We eventually feel the pain of our consequences. He can just wait for us to call Him (yet, He is there every moment ready to help).

3. Using our creative talents and implementing the moral truths of The Ten Commandments will lead most of us to achieve a higher level of success in business, career, relationships with family and others. It is the foundation for satisfying the customer and serving our employees. Unfortunately, they are very hard to completely live by because of the deceit and pressure placed on us in the world. That is why we need more importantly to live by His spiritual principles first.

4. Many of us would say, "Isn't that enough? I believe in God and even call on Him when I really need Him. I'm a good person." But I believe God is saying, "No, that is not enough. I have blessed you in many ways and want to love you more through a personal and spiritual relationship. I have greater plans for your life than being just a moral person." Two out of three is not good enough.

5. God says, "Don't worship the wrong things. There is an eternity beyond this world that I have placed you in and I want the joy of leading you to a higher purpose and more

fulfilling life here and beyond."

6. To come to Me, I need you to be humble like a little child, seeking My face and My word and I will reveal a new life to you forever and ever."

7. All righteous dreams or visions for businesses, careers, missions are inspired by the spirit of God. The closer we come to know Him, the easier we will recognize and understand them. God will anoint people to accomplish His righteous purposes.

8. Every time we follow the Lord's command, we please Him and something happens which blesses us. When we disobey His truths, something negative happens – maybe not immediately, almost as if we are given a "grace period" sometimes, but eventually something 'snaps'. Why? Because we are spiritual people first. He doesn't have to raise a hand, it's the system and eternal truths, commands, and laws that He designed into our lives. We can't just obey some truths, pick and choose our favorite to receive "fullness of joy" in life. However, if we just follow the first and second commandments, (Have no other God before me or false idols.), our hearts will begin to change. That change will lead us to be receptive to all other truths.

"God honors most those who honor Him and His ways."

Final Point:

All problems are rooted in missing the mark God has intended for us while our joy and peace stem from keeping His truths.

BIBLIOGRAPHY

Introduction
American Bible Society, NY, NY

Chapter 1
- Dave Draveky, Hope in the Midst of Adversity, Life Story, Sumas, Washington, 1994
- J. C. Penney, Man with a Thousand Partners, Harper, NY, NY, 1931
- Ben Franklin, The Art of Virtue, George Rogers, Acorn Publishing, Eden Prairie, Minn. 1990
- Truett Cathy, Serving the Lord in Business, Focus on the Family, Colorado Springs, CO 1992
- Martin Luther King, Jr. Martin Luther King, Jr. Companion, St. Martin's Press, NY 1995
- Rick DeVos, Compassionate Capitalism, a Plume Book, Penguin Group, NY, NY 1993
- John Wooden, "My First Seven Points," Fellowship of Christian Athletes, Kansas City, MO, 1990
- Joe Gibbs, "The Proof's in the Power," FCA, Kansas City, MO, 1990
- Character Training Institute, 520 W. Main, Oklahoma City, OK 73102

Chapter 3
- Sam Walton, On My Honor, I Will, Randy Pennington & Marc Bockman, Treasure House Shippenstary, PA 1995
- Orville Redenbacher, "The Funny Looking Farmer with the Funny Sounding Name," Guidepost, NY, NY Jan. 1990
- Bob Nourse, Origins of The Executive Committee (TEC), Milwaukee, WI 1990
- Mary Kay, Mary Kay You Can Have it All, Prima Publishers, Rocklin, CA 1995
- John D. Rockefeller, Rockefeller Billions, Jewel Abels, MacMillan, NY, 1965
- Bill Pollard, The Soul of the Firm, Co-Published Harper Business and Zondervan, Division of Harper Collins Publishers, 1996
- Joe Gibbs, "A Game Plan for Life," Life Story, Sumas, Washington, 1995

Chapter 4
- Frederick Phillips, "Business Ethics for True Profitability," Executive Leadership Foundation, Atlanta, GA 1992
- Ronald Reagan, <u>Speaking My Mind</u>, Simon & Schuster, N.Y., 1989
- Washington, "America's Godly Heritage," Wallbuilders Press, Aledo, Texas, 1992
- Ted Koppel, "The Last Word at Duke University," ABC News, 1987

Chapter 5
- Dr. Laura Nash, <u>Believers in Business</u>, Thomas Nelson Publishers, Nashville, TN 1994
- Richard Hagberg "Rambos in Pinstripes: Why so Many CEOs are Lousy Leaders "Fortune Magazine, Chicago, IL June 24, 1996
- Bob Bowerman, "The Kitchen - Table Shoemaker," Guidepost, January, 1988, NY, NY
- James L. Kraft, "Pattern for Prosperity," Guidepost, N.Y., N.Y. 1954

Chapter 6
- Mary Kay, <u>Mary Kay You Can Have it All</u>, ibid.
- "Abraham Lincoln, Success & Failure," Louis E. Boone, Quotable Business, Random House, New York, 1992
- Jack Stack, <u>Great Game of Business</u>, TEC, Florida, 1994
- John F. Love, <u>McDonald's Behind the Arches</u>, Bantam Books, NY 1995
- Bobby Bowden, "Coach as Christian," Living Words, Jacksonville, FL 1991
- Pete Maravich, "There is Life after the NBA," FCA, Kansas City, MO
- Charles Colson, <u>Thank God for Watergate</u>, Life Story, Sumas, Washington, 1993
- Ronald Reagan, <u>Speaking My Mind</u>, Simon & Schuster, NY, 1989

Chapter 7
- Robert Schuller, <u>Believe in the God Who Believes in You</u>, Thomas Nelson, Nashville, TN 1989
- Dr. Ken Cooper, <u>It's Better to Believe</u>, Thomas Nelson, Nashville, TN 1995
- <u>Love or Perish, None of these Diseases</u>, S.I. McMillen, M.D. Revell, Grand Rapids, MI, Revised 1995

Chapter 8

- Grant Teaff, "Finding God's Will in a Plane Crash," FCA, Kansas City, MO
- Robert Schuller, Believe in the God Who Believes in You, ibid.
- Pete Maravich, "There is Life After the NBA," ibid.
- Dr. Ken Cooper, It's Better to Believe, ibid.
- Tom Landry, FCA, Kansas City, MO 1986
- Bobby Bowden, "Coach as a Christian," ibid.
- Ken Blanchard, We are the Beloved, Zondervan Publishing, Grand Rapids, MI 1994
- George Herman, "Babe Ruth," New Guidepost, 1954, edited by Norman Vincent Peale

Chapter 9

- J. C. Penney, 50 Years of the Golden Rule, Harper & Row, NY, 1950
- Cecil B. deMille, "How Faith Learned as a Boy Guided My Career," Guidepost, N.Y., NY. 1954
- Mary Kay, Mary Kay, You Can Have it All, ibid.
- Jessie Shwayder, Samsonite Corporation, On My Honor, I Will, ibid.
- Julius Erving, FCA, Kansas City, MO 1986
- Richard Kughn, "Like a Kid in a Candy Store," Guidepost, N.Y., N.Y., December 1990

Chapter 10

- Adolph Coors, IV, No Right to Hate, Voice Speaks About, Gift Publications, Costa Mesa, CA 1989
- Jim Moran, Florida Chamber News, Florida Chamber of Commerce, Tallahassee, FL, March, 1996
- Tom Watson, Caring, The Book of Business Anecdotes, Peter Hay, Wing Books, Avenel, N.J., 1988
- Robert Townsend, Further up the Organization
- Homer Figler," My Minister Meant Business," Guidepost, NY, NY, April, 1984
- Sam Walton, Sam Walton Made in America, Bantam Audio Publishing, NY, NY, 1992

Chapter 11

- Lee Ezell,"Answers to Life's Missing Pieces," Life Story, Sumas, Wash. 1995

How to get Rich... By the Book

- Charlie & Dotty Duke, "Walk on the Moon, Walk with the Son," Sumas, Wash. 1993
- Michelle Quinn, "Today's CEO: Focused, Domineering, Tireless," San Jose Mercury News, San Jose, CA, June 24, 1996
- Manville Quote: On My Honor I Will, ibid.
- Jack Eckerd, Finding the Right Prescription, JME, Clearwater, FL 1987

Chapter 12

- John D. Rockefeller, None of the Diseases, ibid.
- Stew Leonard, Why Smart People Do Dumb Things, Mortimer Feinberg, Ph.D. and John J. Tarrant, Fireside, NY, NY 1995
- "International Pirating," Wall Street Journal, Dow Jones Corp, NY, NY, April 20, 1996
- Wally Amos, "The Calling Card," Guideposts, NY, NY, March 1985
- Bill Pollard, The Soul of the Firm, ibid.

Chapter 13

- Frank Abagnale, Catch Me if You Can, Focus on the Family, Colorado Springs, CO 1993
- Beechnut, The Taming of the Shrewd, Paul DeVries and Barry Gardner, Thomas Nelson, Nashville, TN, 1992
- David Schwartz, "Truth - It's Good Business," Guideposts, NY, NY, January 1985
- Abraham Lincoln, The Book of Anecdotes, ibid.
- Ken Wessner, The Soul of the Firm, ibid.

Chapter 14

- Jackie Robinson, "Trouble Ahead Needn't Bother You," Guideposts Book, NY, NY 1954
- Pricie Hanna, "The New Vice President," Guidepost, NY, NY, August 1986
- Bill Cosby, C-Span, Viewer Services, Washington, DC, April 8, 1996
- Andy Story, Believers in Business, Dr. Laura Nash, ibid.

Chapter 15

- J. C. Penney, David F. Miller used with permission, 1987

Illustrations

- Many quotes from <u>God's Little Illustration Book</u>, Honor Book, Tulsa, OK 1993
- Some Quotes from <u>God's Lite Chicken Soup for the Spirit</u>
- William D. Lawrence with Jack A. Turpin, <u>Beyond the Bottom Line</u>, Praxis Books, Moody Press, Chicago, 1994

APPENDIX

What Do We Worship?

As long as man and woman have existed on earth they have sought an idol or god to worship to fill their own "spiritual vacuum." In psychological terms, it is a need to find a source of security...a place to rest, feel comfort, call home, a place to hide from the unknowns of life, be fulfilled...our rock and anchor. We seek those places to draw meaning and purpose, find identity, to overcome our fears and doubts about the unknown, things we don't understand and need to "make sense." It is the longing to find something that fills the "vacuum" that God placed in each of us.

In the days of the Old Testament many created statues, golden calves, while others worshiped the sun, the wind or the earth and called them gods. In the American society, based on Christian Biblical principles, we have experienced the greatest prosperity in the shortest period of time of any other nation on earth. So many of us are easily deceived, ignorant or become too "intelligent" to fall for a "story of a savior dying on a cross," or being "saved" from what? Don't we already have the good life?

Most of us have picked or chosen a variety of _false idols_ to worship, to fill the inner need we experience. The Bible refers to them in different passages and they are most often recognized as the "Seven Sins of the Heart." Here are the examples below:

FALSE IDOLS

Problem:	The "spiritual vacuum" causes us to seek false idols which we become entrapped into worshiping.
Causes:	Insecurities, deceit, fear, seeds of pain in the heart, bad habits, wrong role model and culture, sins of parents.
Outward Confirmations:	Denial defensiveness, blaming others, physical appearance, habits.

Healing: Admitting a problem, prayer (asking for help), immersion in the Word of God, counseling, fellowship, support, acts of God and the Holy Spirit, forgiveness, and love, love and love...through a personal relationship with Christ.

1. *Pride/Egotism* — is a belief in one's self characterized by *"whatever I earn I get," "I'm number one,"* the self-made man/woman, *"you can be anything you want to be," "I am woman, I am strong," "I control my own destiny," "I am my own man,"* and *"I did it my way."* Being proud of your family, business, friends is fine. If we use our God-given talents to get ahead or to become successful without recognizing Him shows a "lack of knowledge and respect." We have, in effect, chosen to say, "I'm my own god." Typically we become self-centered, concerned about being right (having all the right answers), wanting always to be in control, or "looking good" and defensive...all characteristics of pride gone too far. It is either arrogance or ignorance apart from God.

2. *Gluttony/Addictions* — This starts with the development of a habit in seeking pleasure As depression or frustration gets worse, the dependency gets stronger. The addiction provides the temporary high for relief. It becomes our "fix" (or god). It is what we worship and can't live without. Since it is spiritually rooted, without God, it is not possible for an individual to overcome their own willpower. Changing to a dependency on God is the only sure source of turnaround. Besides drugs, alcohol, smoking, and food, there are a number of other addictions we might seek, i.e., work, TV, being a sports fanatic, or even simple things like shopping, golf, tennis, fishing. Some of these areas are fine if we keep them in balance and not allow them to come before our relationship with God, family or friends.

3. *Anger* — is either inherited, taught by parents or learned through seed words of bitterness, hate, or jealousy which take

Appendix - What Do We Worship?

root in the spirit, build up and finally have to be released. Anger is released through yelling or violent acts. Anger can be a defensive mode where we fight back from being hurt. The deep rooted bitterness or hate in the heart can only be cured through the healing power of the word of God and His Love. Psychological counseling might help but seldom gets to the root of spiritual damage without Him.

4. *Lust* — for power, possessions or sexual release are the most common. Sexual desire for a man is a craving and crying out for love. Men more than women express love through the sexual act. It is a way to fill a spiritual void and hurt. It becomes such a passion through mental pictures; that is why pornography, suggestive TV commercials and clubs fuel the problem.

5. *Laziness* — is the lack of motivation from little or no faith in themselves or the true God. While this can relate to physical energy, it has more to do with the "grip" on the heart than the mind. It is an avoidance of pain, avoiding the fear of failure with other people. Sleep, T.V., and food are ways to avoid reality and not having to deal with the fear inside. To God it is waste of talent and love.

6. *Envy* — is learned from parents and the world's false images. It is a hiding place for a damaged heart. People find comfort in "pity parties," wallowing in the hurt they feel of being deprived, short-changed in life. They become paralyzed in their dreams and desires to have what others have and allow bitterness to become resentment for others. It is fueled with gossip and breeds more jealousy and hurt.

7. *Greed* — becomes a craving or passion to create a sense of self-worth in an individual. Without it they consider themselves failures and they measure others by it. At the same time, it creates an imbalance in a person's life because their god can destroy a marriage, family, friendship or a

business. Money cannot buy anything eternal. Some take it on so deeply that they believe it is a purpose for their life. God gives some people talent to create capital and wealth, just as he gives an athlete great ability but if they live their life for this one master, it destroys their spirit.

Many deprived children have taken on the god of money as a way to overcome the hurt that remains in their heart from the "underdog mentality," while others catch the sickness from their parents' attitudes. God wants many of us to be successful financially, but He also wants us to give back. To whom much is given, much is required.. Unless you want to be buried in your Cadillac, money will do you no good after your death.

These false gods create a situation of trying to serve two masters. He created us to only serve Him. Our physical, mental and spiritual makeup is designed this way. We need His help to overcome any false gods which entrap us in a world of deceit.

Appendix - What Do We Worship?

THE 14 ETERNAL TRUTHS THAT DETERMINE RICHES

The Truth - The first four truths were revealed at creation. The next ten, Moses shared with the Jews who hungered for direction and a fulfilling new life. As parents, we lay down the law, "Don't run into the street." A stop or speed limit sign are directions for our conduct. God's Truths are signs for success and danger.

The Spirit of the Truth - is the why, how, and what to do of each Truth. Jesus brought and modeled the Spirit of Truth in the New Testament. The "spirit" of every contract has an intent or deeper application beyond the written word. So it is with God's Truths. He looks at our motive, actions and obedience in relationship to them.

Character Quality - As the first Truth illustrates, He wants us to take on His character. Each truth has an application to bring us closer to His purposes, character and righteousness.

Forgiveness - is required by God. Matthew 6:14-15 says, "If you won't forgive others, you offend God's creation, thus offending Him. He will not forgive you." Matthew 7:12 says, "So in everything, do to others what you would have them to do to you, for this sums up the law and the prophets." (The Golden Rule)

Appendix - The 14 Eternal Truths That Determine Riches

	THE TRUTH *Genesis 1:26* *(paraphrased)*	**THE SPIRIT OF THE TRUTH**	**CHARACTER QUALITY**
I.	God created man in His own image.	• I created you in love, grace and to be righteous. • To love and be loved. • To be kind and patient. • To be accountable and forgiving. • To be a light to others. • To love and enjoy life. • Think long term. • Jesus came to model My character. • Learn from your trials.	Take on My character of Love.
II.	Be fruitful and increase in numbers.	• To multiply, reproduce, profit. • To plant, nurture, harvest. • To create, discover and enjoy. • To grow personally and share with others. • To learn and respect the use of My resources.	Sow, grow, and reap.
III.	Fill the earth and subdue it.	• To plan, delegate, build, control. • To take initiative, be aggressive and do your best • To use your personality, intelligence, skills, natural desires. • To witness, carry My name to the ends of the earth.	Put your talents to work.
IV.	Rule over/every living creature.	• To make laws, lead, be responsible for truth. • To communicate, teach, and be an example. • To establish principles and rules to live by. • To be tough when necessary in love and sacrifice.	Lead by example.

Creation Truths
We are given dominion and asked to take initiative, yet created to need God. He keeps spiritual controls of heaven and earth.

201

How to get Rich... By the Book

	THE TRUTH The Ten Commandments Deuteronomy 5:6-21 (paraphrased)	THE SPIRIT OF THE TRUTH The New Testament (paraphrased) *Jesus said, "Love your God with all your heart and all your might."*	CHARACTER QUALITY
1.	Have no other Gods before me.	• Love me as your God, put Me first in your life and I will fill your spirit and give you visions. • Be open and humble to My leading. • Pride before Me will cause emptiness, stress and unfruitfulness. • Only I, as your creator, know your needs. • Worry not, put your trust in Me.	Be humble and trust Me.
2.	Have no false idols.	• As God, I am spirit, love, truth and light. • I am not represented by superstitions, statues, people, material wealth or physical objects. • I am a jealous God, so heed My words. • Generations will be effected by your love for Me. • No one can serve two masters, watch what you worship.	Be convicted and forgiven.
3.	Don't use God's name in vain.	• Honor Me with thanksgiving, praise, and prayer. • My name is Holy and commands power. • Preserve My name in the hearts of your people. • Your words create and command good and evil. • Life and death is in the power of the tongue.	Praise with your tongue.
4.	Keep the Sabbath holy.	• Plan to rest and spend time with Me. • My word, prayer and fellowship will teach you. • Love, peace, joy and wisdom will come to those who grow close to Me.	Rest and listen in Me.

Spiritual Truths Toward God
Spiritual truths are about a personal relationship with the Lord, and about doing His will.

Appendix - The 14 Eternal Truths That Determine Riches

	THE TRUTH	**THE SPIRIT OF THE TRUTH** Jesus said, "secondly, love your neighbor as yourself." (Referred to also as "The Golden Rule")	**CHARACTER QUALITY**
5.	Honor your father and mother.	• Love, honor and forgive your mother, father, spouse and children because they represent My plan for families and organizations. • Every organization is a family where authority should be respected, honored and followed. • Pray for those in authority.	Respect authority as family.
6.	You shall not murder.	• Build relationships with others. • Love your fellowman, no matter how he offends you. • Life and death is My decision, not yours. • Forgiveness will heal your heart.	Forgive and value life.
7.	You shall not commit adultery.	• Love and be fruitful to those you have joined in covenant. • Abstain from impure relationships until commitment, true love, for My purposes. • Honor your employer and employees with love, respect and fairness.	Be faithful and loyal.
8.	You shall not steal.	• Give to others and it will be given unto you. • I will bless you bountifully for loving and protecting your fellowman. • Tithe to prove your love to Me. • Your motive will be judged.	Give to others.
9.	Do not bear false witness.	• Respect your fellowman by being honest with him in all things. • Communicate with integrity, do not withhold truth. • Be open to listen with discernment for I will use your fellowman to confirm My intentions.	Earn respect and integrity through honesty.
10.	You shall not covet the goods of others.	• Pray that your fellowman and his family will be richly blessed, prosper and grow without regard to your desires. • I will provide for your needs according to My plan. • Every man's talents, skills, abilities, personality, and physical features will be different and have unique rewards.	Appreciate and encourage others.

Moral Truth Toward Man
Moral truths between you and your fellowman will affect the continued success of any family or organization.

Index of People

Frank Abagnale 153	Homer Figler 122
John Adams 42, 46	Ben Franklin 4, 32, 41
Alfred Adler 84	Willie Gary 28
Wally Amos 146	Joe Gibbs 10, 34, 175
Walter Anderson 93	Bill Gothard 12
Maya Angelou 158	Nadine Gramling 57
Bill Aronson 155	Rich Hagberg 56
Jim Bakker 75	Pricie Hanna 171
Charles Barkley 6	Karen Hanson 167
David Barton 43	Bob Harrison 56
Ken Blanchard 12, 58, 94	James Haskett 33
Smiley Blanton 84	Tom Hill 11
Bobby Bowden 55, 70, 99	Sadam Hussein 44
Bob Bowerman 58	Grant Jefferies 26
Bennett Brown 156	Clark Johnson 124, 156
Bob Buford 95	Herb Johnson 121
Jim Brewer 7, 15	Mary Kay 31, 65, 110
Tony Campolo 112	Pat Kelly 69, 148
Andrew Carnegie 146	Martin Luther King 6
Truett Cathy 5, 100	Phil Knight 58
Chuck Colson 72	Dr. Kolb 85
Jamie Colter 75	Ted Koppel 43
Dr. Ken Cooper 82, 96	James Kraft 59
Adolph Coors IV 117	Ray Kroc 68
Bill Cosby 172	Richard Kughn 112
Jim Coté 108	Tom Landry 99
Rich DeVos 9	Bernhard Langer 99
Cecil B. de Mille 109	Doug Leatherdale 82
Alexis deToqueville 42	Rob Lebow 174
Walt Disney 70	Stew Leonard 145
Jim Dobson 174	Robert Levering 135
Dave Dravecky 3	Abraham Lincoln 40, 66, 154
Peter Drucker 139	Frank Maguire 18
Charles and Dorothy Duke 136	Pete Maravich 72, 96
Albert Einstein 146	Maurice Mascarenhas 120
Dwight Eisenhower 17, 44	Charles Mayo 82
Jack Eckerd 138	Bill McCartney 27, 51, 149
Julius Erving 111	Bill McCombes 98
Lee Ezell 131	S.I. McMillen 83

How to get Rich... By the Book

David Miller 181-186
Jim Miller 7, 110
Norm Miller 108
Marilyn Monroe 133
Jim Moran 118
Sister Helen Mrosla 79
Ralph Nader 159
Laura Nash 52, 173
Richard Nixon 155
Alfred Nobel 68
Bob Nourse 31
Bill Oncken 19
Tom Osborne 11, 99
Sen. Bob Packwood 132
Blaise Pascal 73
Pope John Paul II 42
J. C. Penney 5, 107, 118, 181-186
Tom Peters 145
Frederick Phillips 39
Tom Phillips 55
Bill Pollard 33, 147
Clint Purvis 35
Ronald Reagan 39, 73
Orville Redenbacher 29
Branch Rickey 165
Jackie Robinson 165
John D. Rockefeller 32, 143, 146
Jim Rohn 31
Theodore Roosevelt 159
Larry Rosen 158
Bob Rosof 11
"Rudy" Ruettiger 28
Babe Ruth 60
Ed Ryan 8, 157
Col. Sanders 70
Judge James Sarokin 136
Charles "Red" Scott 8, 57
John Scott 53
Dr. Robert Schuller 35, 80, 83, 93
Dave Schwartz 157

Dean Sherman 52
Jesse Shwayder 111
Johnny Simmons 167
Charles Smith 53
Jack Stack 68, 123
E. Stern, MD 83
Gil Stricklin 100
Grant Teaff 91
Mother Teresa 95, 96
Carl Terzian 159
Dr. Robert Thompson 21
Robert Townsend 122
Brian Tracey 53, 83
Mark Twain 155
Jay Van Andel 9
Michael H. Walsh 59
Don Walker 156
Sam Walton 8, 29, 118
George Washington 41
Tom Watson 68, 121
Ken Wessner 160
Reggie White 7
George Williams 168
John Wooden 9, 29, 121

Appendix - Final Word

THE BEGINNING STEPS TO GETTING RICH BY THE BOOK

God knows your heart and is not so concerned with your words as He is with the attitude of your heart. The following is a suggested prayer:

> *"Lord Jesus, I need You. Thank You for dying on the cross for my sins. I open the door of my life and receive You as my Savior and Lord. Thank You for forgiving my sins and giving me eternal life. Take control of the throne of my life. Make me the kind of person You want me to be."*

SUGGESTIONS FOR CHRISTIAN GROWTH

Spiritual growth results from trusting Jesus Christ. "The righteous man shall live by faith." (Galatians 3:11) A life of faith will enable you to trust God increasingly with every detail of your life, and to practice the following:

- **G**   Go to God in prayer daily (John 15:7).
- **R**   Read God's Word daily (Acts 17:11)—begin with the Gospel of John.
- **O**   Obey God moment by moment (John 14:21).
- **W**   Witness for Christ by your life and words (Matthew 4:19; John 15:8).
- **T**   Trust God for every detail of your life (1 Peter 5:7).
- **H**   Holy Spirit - allow Him to control and empower your daily life and witness (Galatians 5:16,17; Acts 1:8).

FELLOWSHIP IN A GOOD CHURCH

God's Word admonishes us not to forsake "the assembling of ourselves together" (Hebrews 10:25). Several logs burn brightly together; but put one aside on the cold hearth and the fire goes out. So it is with your relationship with other Christians. If you do not belong to a church, do not wait to be invited. Take the initiative; call the pastor of a nearby church where Christ is honored and His Bible is taught. Start this week, and make plans to attend regularly.

Reprinted from The Four Spiritual Laws, Campus Crusade for Christ.

Appendix - Final Word

ABOUT THE AUTHOR

John F. Beehner is an entrepreneur, having started four different businesses. His 12 years as founder and CEO of TEC Florida (The Executive Committee) afforded him a rare opportunity to individually work with over one hundred different CEOs of small to mid-size companies. The process focuses on peer advisory groups and individual feedback sessions while capitalizing on the experiences and knowledge of hundreds of outside experts and CEOs as speakers.

John's spiritual journey began in 1982 and led him to the TEC business. In 1995, he received a vision to combine his practical business experience with the insight he received through prayer and scripture. John believes his experience of strategy, motivation, marketing and management combined with the insight of purpose, peace, love and success, will help executives understand God's design for a rapidly changing world hungry for the Truth.

In 1995, he sold his majority interest in TEC to pursue the publication of this book.

By the Book Publishing is dedicated to help business executives understand the spiritual principles which affect their individual performance and company's success through small group workshops. For further information regarding book orders, or if you are interested in contributing stories for future publications, please telephone, 1 (888) 847-3861.